One Heart Too Many

Facing the Challenges of Loving a Widower

DENISE MEDANY

ISBN: 0692132627
ISBN-13: 978-0692132623

DEDICATION

This book is dedicated to the women who make the necessary sacrifices to offer unconditional love, even in the most difficult of circumstances.

CONTENTS

ACKNOWLEDGMENTS

I would like to thank my mother for teaching me how to stand up for myself, and my father, whose passion I inherited. I would like to thank my editor, Beth Bruno, who went above and beyond. Her encouragement and confidence is greatly appreciated. I would also like to thank the women who contributed to this book and trusted me to share their most private thoughts, feelings, and experiences. Last but not least, I would like to thank my son, who shares my proclivity for battling injustice. His assistance helped make my dream of writing this book a reality.

INTRODUCTION

This book has been a long time coming. It's about the type of relationship that does not get the recognition and respect it deserves. Although the focus of this book is geared toward women in a relationship with a widower, the same principles also apply to men who love a widow.

I have always been someone people seek out for advice. Several years ago, at the urging of many, many people, I began writing a generic relationship-based book. As it evolved, it became geared toward women who were getting back into the dating scene later in life. More and more, however, I found that the majority of women who were gravitating toward me in my research were those who were involved with widowers. It consumed such a huge part of what I was writing that I deleted much of what was in the book and decided to completely devote my efforts to the challenges of being involved with a widower. I realized that there weren't many books written on this subject for women by a woman. Almost all of the widow- or widower-related books out there are for those who are trying to put the pieces of their lives back together after the death of their spouses; only a few of them mention the perspectives of the women who get involved with widowers.

In no way do I want to create the impression that I am a therapist or a professional counselor. Except for a keen interest in human behavior, I have had no formal education or experience in the field of psychology. I do, however, have a master's degree from the School of Hard Knocks. I firmly believe that nobody can better understand the challenges faced by others than one who has walked the same path. In that spirit, I wrote this book to offer what I have learned from my own involvement with a widower, as well as from other women who have entered loving relationships with a man who has lost his wife.

In the chapters that follow, I offer my personal opinions along with the thoughts and feelings of the women I've interviewed about the different facets of the complicated issues I have discovered during my research. Human emotions are complex and it is my hope that by shedding light and awareness on a type of relationship that has been given very little exposure, it might help to create some understanding and compassion for those involved.

I have not come across many books written from a woman's perspective that address the various struggles that women face — in vivid detail — when getting involved with a widower. There are self-help books on the market for every other relationship issue under the sun. Women who get involved with widowers are a large but unrecognized and underappreciated group that deserves support and validation.

Many kinds of pain accompany the loss of a partner and I have experienced that pain. As a widow engaged to a widower, I understand the death of a spouse. I have also been divorced. In my conversations with a number of women from various walks of life, I have discovered that while the ages, geographical locations, and dynamics are different, there is one strong common denominator: loving a man whose previous marriage or relationship ended in death is probably one of the most difficult and emotionally taxing situations these women have ever been in.

This book takes a pragmatic "take no prisoners" approach to widower-related challenges. We all have different levels of tolerance; what might be acceptable to one woman could be an absolute deal breaker for another. There is no "one size fits all" set of conditions, but rather, the belief that one has to determine if what is being given to them is proportionately reciprocal before deciding whether or not a relationship is going to work. This is a basic standard that can be applied to ALL areas of life.

As I mentioned earlier, I am a widow myself, having lost my husband to a sudden, tragic and unexpected death. I am also currently engaged to a widower, so in my experience, as a person who has been on both sides of the fence, I must say that being a widowed person is far easier than being involved with one; therefore, my loyalty and support is for the women involved with men whose marriages ended due to the death of their wives. There is no other relationship where a woman is expected to embrace a large part of her partner's history with another woman or accept conditions that would be considered deal breakers in other relationships. I will describe many different scenarios that others have shared with me during many long and detailed conversations and interviews with those who have walked this path. Hopefully, my discussions with these women will shed light on relationship issues that do not get enough respect or exposure elsewhere.

Everybody is sympathetic to the needs and feelings of the bereaved, especially the surviving spouse of a woman who has passed away, yet they often give little thought to the woman who was unknowingly drawn into a relationship with the widower following that loss. It's a natural assumption that when a widower starts dating, he has fully recovered from the death of his wife and is ready to leave the past behind and move on. If this is not the case, then his actions may be construed as deceptive and misleading; therefore, the new woman may become the injured party because she was drawn into a widower's life under false pretenses. All she wanted was to be in a meaningful relationship with a nice guy. Instead, she is dragged into the remnants of another woman's life and expected to adjust to potentially intolerable conditions with long-suffering patience. She may be perceived to be a heartless, cold-blooded shrew who lacks compassion for the bereaved widower she loves. The worst part is that the woman may already be emotionally invested in her relationship with the widower before she realizes that he is still strongly attached to his late wife. This may cause her unspeakable frustration and disillusionment.

I wrote the following poem as a compilation that sums up the most common and often repeated feelings of women who are in love with widowers.

"Ode to the Widower"

To men who have been widowed,
we understand your pain.
But you have a right to love again,
without having to explain.

It's true that life as you knew it,
came to a very sad end.
Your late wife has passed away,
but it's time for your heart to mend.

It was normal to wonder about many things
as the days and weeks went by
Would you ever feel happy and normal again?
Why did she have to die?

I'm sure there were many sad thoughts
that were running through your head
But you must be strong, get back on track
and stop focusing on the one who is dead!

There were surely many adjustments
but not such a big surprise
to realize you need to get rid of her things,
and say your final goodbyes.

Your misery will be lifted
if you choose to stop feeling sad.
Quit thinking about what was taken away
and the life that you once had

Time heals all wounds, you know
and with that comes relief
If you truly want to be happy again
you must let go of all your grief

Your burden will be lifted
and your world no longer strange
Your happy spirit will return
when you accept what you can't change

Everybody experiences heartache
during the natural course of life
You shouldn't expect special treatment
just because you lost your wife

You cannot enjoy the relationship we're in
if you keep dwelling on the past
You must decide to move ahead
to make our new love last

You have a wonderful woman today
who loves being part of your life
but you must give me your entire heart
I won't share it with your late wife

Appreciate your life with me
You're lucky to get a second chance
I want to be with you at your side
To love, laugh and do a happy dance

Make no mistake, I'm not a fool
Don't use me to ease your pain
You'll discover that you've lost my love
during your strolls down Memory Lane

There is a choice to make, you see
Life can really be quite fine
Stop the torchbearing activities
If you truly want to be mine

I've been more patient than I should have been
But now it's time to choose
If you don't act soon, I'll decide for you
and you're the one who will lose

There is no room for three people
I doubt that's what you prefer
You cannot hold on to both of us
It's either me or her

Don't display her belongings
I refuse to live in a shrine
Our home must reflect your life with ME
that's the bottom line!

Vows aren't good forever
... only 'til death do you part
Embrace the love you have for me
And I'll give you all of my heart

There are many relationship-based books on the market today, such as how to find the love of your life; how to recover from a breakup or the loss of a spouse and get back in the dating game; how to put that spark back into your relationship; and how to land the one who got away. But when it comes to finding books about loving and living with a widower, the pickings are painfully slim. Women who love such a man are the unsung heroes who, for too long, have suffered in silence. My intention is to give a loud, bold voice to the many brave women who dare to take the risks and challenges of stepping into another woman's life.

As I will repeatedly point out, many widowers do not realize the full extent of their grief. They think they have worked though the worst of it and are ready to find a new relationship. More often than not, this is not the case.

Let's face it: the only time people are happy to be single again is after they've broken free of a relationship that made them absolutely miserable. It's difficult to fly solo after being coupled for so many years, and the difficulty is compounded for the widower whose late wife died suddenly and unexpectedly, as he had no time to get himself emotionally prepared, no opportunity to say the things he wanted to say or to get certain affairs in order. His entire life as he knew it came to an abrupt end without any warning or closure. Even in the case where his late wife had a lingering illness and her death was anticipated, the widower may have been so busy trying to cope and manage everything that he didn't have a chance to think about what was coming. When his wife finally dies, everything comes to a complete stop — literally. There are no more trips back and forth to doctors or hospitals, no more picking up prescriptions or sitting with his wife while her condition progressively worsens. On top of all this, the husband may have been running back and forth to his job and trying to stay strong for the sake of the children and other loved ones. This frenzy of activity ceases when his wife finally passes away.

Whether the death was sudden or anticipated, the widower is surrounded by friends, family, and neighbors, all trying to provide support and comfort. People stay close by to help with the arrangements, household chores, pets, and other responsibilities that require ongoing attention. The widower does not feel the full impact of his loss until later. As with any death, everybody goes back to their own lives after the funeral, and this is when the magnitude of the loss hits him the hardest. There is nothing left for him to do except to think about how the rest of his life is going to unfold. He is in unfamiliar territory and a lifestyle that is foreign to him. His late wife's absence becomes more conspicuous than ever. This is the point where he starts trying to put the pieces of his life back together and, more often than not, his way of making things right for himself is to jump into a new relationship.

1. THE NEW RELATIONSHIP

You met a wonderful man. He makes it known that he is neither a player, nor is he interested in casual dating. He wants to be in a relationship. He is looking for exclusivity. He's friendly, charming, and well-mannered. He loves spending time with you. He is also a widower. Your first thought is, "Wow, what a catch! Here is a good, solid, family man who knows how to stay in a marriage 'til death do you part'. He seems like he could be everything I ever wanted." Um — not so fast!

At first, everything is wonderful. You love the way he speaks so beautifully about his late wife. It's such a refreshing change from the anger and bitterness you sometimes see in divorced men. Your widower puts his late wife on a pedestal, even after her death. He is attached to her memory with the kind of devotion that you greatly admire. You find yourself fantasizing about how wonderful it would be to be loved with that same degree of intensity. You're filled with high hopes; you're optimistic about the relationship potential. He has already proven to be a solid, stable husband right up until the very end. If he can love his late wife that much, it's a good indication that he has the capacity to love YOU the same way. You SO want that kind of love for yourself and here is the man who has the potential to give it to you.

You want to know all about his late wife. The way they met, how he proposed to her, the life they led, the kind of marriage they had, and what caused her death. You listen in rapt fascination as he talks about her non-stop. He never gets tired of telling you about her and you never get tired of listening, wanting to know as much as you can find out about the woman who had such a hold on his heart.

You're on a pink cloud.

Unfortunately, things aren't moving along in the way you had hoped. After a while, you grow tired of hearing about his late wife. It's getting old.

He isn't showing any indication that he's moving forward with you. He's so busy looking back on his life with her that he doesn't seem to recognize or fully appreciate who and what is right in front of him. You're starting to wonder if his main focus will ever shift away from her and on to you.

This phase of the relationship is frustrating. You are progressively becoming more and more of a regular couple, yet you aren't established enough to have a firm place in his life. You don't feel like you've earned the right to speak up, so you do your best to be patient and understanding while he finds his way. He is, after all, new at this. You find it endearing that he's inexperienced and a bit clumsy at the dating game as a result of being out of circulation for so long. You're also happy that he met you while he's still so out of practice. He's not bitter or jaded in any way from a nasty breakup. You love that he's not a seasoned player, yet you're becoming impatient for what you know you can have after he's ready to move on.

The smoke is starting to clear and reality is setting in.

It's been said that after becoming widowed, women grieve but men replace. What that means is that most widowed women will recoil from the very thought of being with another man. She misses her late husband and she can't even imagine putting herself back out there again. She leans on family and friends for support and comfort.

Widowers, on the other hand, deal with their pain differently. They are accustomed to being married; there is a gaping hole in their lives that needs filling. They don't cry on their buddies' shoulders. Their way of dealing with a loss like this is to jump into another relationship shockingly soon after their wives pass away, long before they have completely recovered from her death. This is what causes a world of trouble. The widower may THINK he's ready for another relationship, but the truth is that he is NOT. He's only ready to fill the void in his life and that's not fair for either party involved.

You're now an established couple. At first, he was reluctant to introduce you to his family and friends out of concern over their reaction to his dating again, but finally he decides to go ahead and do it.

This is where the trouble starts.

You're beginning to meet the people in his life. If you're the first woman he's been with since his late wife died, you may be subjected to a lot of resentment and hostility from his children. You take the high road because, after all, they're still grieving the loss of their mother. Your presence causes an unwelcome fear that the mother they loved and lost is replaceable to their father. The former in-laws are also a part of the picture because they are, after all, still the children's relatives. They, too, might resent your presence, as it only reinforces the fact that their loved one is gone and her husband is moving on. They don't want her to be forgotten and you're the intruder who is erasing her essence.

It's not just the family, either. Let's talk about his friends — the couples whom your widower and his late wife used to socialize with. They're happy for your widower. It's great to see him smiling again, and they love that he can now rejoin them in their couples-oriented activities. Even if they are nice and accepting of you, it's hard to listen as they talk about people, places, and events that they all shared as a group before you came along. You feel segregated. You might hear how thrilled they are for the two of you, and that it's nice to see their widower friend happy again. They'll tell you about his late wife, what a wonderful person she was, and how much you would have loved her. While their words may be well intended, it's all starting to make you feel like you're simply a necessary placeholder filling an unwanted vacancy.

In some cases, you may feel a slight distance from the friends. It's only natural that they scrutinize you and silently compare you to the woman your widower was once married to. They may never admit it, but that's what they're doing.

At the start of your relationship, you missed all these signs. They were there, but let's face it, you BOTH put your best foot forward because you were, after all, auditioning for a relationship. Your widower, unfamiliar with his new role as a single man, wasn't sure what to say and do, so he just droned on and on about his late wife, thinking nothing of it. It's only natural for people to tell each other all about themselves while they're still getting to know each other, but a widower can't tell you much about just himself because so much of his life included his late wife.

Wishing to be supportive and to avoid looking shallow, you listen with rapt fascination and sympathy as he spills his guts about the pain of losing her. There is a tolerant smile pasted on your face as you hear all about his wonderful memories of her. You haven't complained because you don't want to appear to be insensitive, and the truth is that you really don't mind — at first. You figure that maybe he's not sure what else to talk about; maybe he's nervous after being out of the dating game for so long and you tell yourself that he'll get her out of his system once you become more familiar with each other and your relationship becomes firmly established. In time, though, the continued mention of the late wife starts to get under your skin, and when you try to explain that to him, he's bewildered because it's all news to him. Not only have you never had a problem with it before, but you also used to ask questions, encouraging him to talk about her. It seems to him that out of the blue, he gets blindsided by your disapproval. What was never a problem before has now become a major bone of contention between the two of you. HE wants to know where all this seemingly sudden resentment came from. YOU want to know why he can't stop dwelling on the past and start looking ahead to a life with you.

2. FRUSTRATION

There are many frustrations for someone who loves a widower. There has been little respect for or credit given to the woman who inadvertently falls in love with a man whose marriage ended because of the death of his wife. There are a lot of obstacles and challenges that don't exist in other relationships. You secretly wonder if those closest to him would prefer to see him grieving forever instead of replacing his late wife and moving on. If that's what you're thinking, stop right there. You're NOT "replacing" the late wife. When she died, that was the end of his story with her. You're a unique individual in your own right, lovable for your own special characteristics. You aren't a replacement. You're the start of a whole new phase that has nothing to do with his previous life. That part of his story is over. It should be all about YOU now.

When two people marry at a relatively young age, they have not had much of a chance to get out there and experience much of life apart from each other. They buy a house, have children, and focus on raising their family. This is the only existence the widower knew. He's happy, comfortable and secure in the world that he has grown accustomed to, then something happens and the wife dies. Suddenly, the widower finds himself yanked out of his comfort zone. He doesn't know how to fly solo and live as a single person. He's not just grieving the death of his wife; he's also mourning the loss of his own life as he knew it. More than anything else, he wants to go back to a familiar routine that makes sense to him. He thinks he's ready to move on, but what he's REALLY ready for is to fill that void in his life. He wants to be in a relationship again. This is where YOU come in.

You may remember the movie *Return to Me*. It's about a happily married man whose wife dies in a tragic automobile accident. He's lost, heartbroken, and inconsolable. His friend tries to get him out by fixing him up on a blind dinner date with a loud, obnoxious woman who is rude to the waitress. The blind date turns out to be such a disaster, that he makes an excuse to end the evening early, but not before the cute, friendly, witty waitress catches his eye. He returns to the restaurant the next day to pick up his cell phone, which he had forgotten in his haste to get away from his unpleasant blind date, and while there he sees that same waitress. He ends up making plans to go out with her, and after one date, he's smitten. The morning after his date with the waitress, he shows up at work in high spirits with a bounce in his step and a sparkle in his eye. His co-workers notice it immediately, as this is a sudden change from the broken man that they've watched him become after his wife died. Things couldn't be better between the widower and his new lady until he discovers that on the same day that his late wife died, his new love had a transplant, receiving the heart of his late wife, who was a registered organ donor. Neither one of them can deal with this ironic twist of fate, and they split up for a time, but they later get back together again and live happily ever after. Sounds romantic, doesn't it? Unfortunately, life doesn't play out like a fairy tale the way it's often portrayed in the movies.

I have spoken to dozens of women who were or have been in a relationship with a widower. In the next several chapters, you will read various stories that many women have shared with me during the course of my research. Some of the names and certain details have been changed in order to protect the anonymity of those I interviewed.

3. DIRTY LITTLE SECRET

After a nasty divorce to a man who had been repeatedly unfaithful to her, Alice was wary and mistrustful of men. She vowed to be much more particular and discerning if and when she decided to start dating again. When finally ready, she signed up with an online dating site and this is how she met Don. They started slowly, exchanging casual emails and phone calls. Both were surprised at how easily the conversation flowed, and it felt natural for them to open up to each other even further. Alice confided in him about the pain and humiliation of being married to a man who cheated on her. Don shared the agony and loneliness of losing his beloved wife, Rita, to cancer eight months earlier, after twenty-six years of marriage. Alice admired his obvious devotion and love for his late wife. He was a refreshing change from the philanderer to whom she had been married. In spite of her determination to take it slow, she found herself falling in love with Don. He seemed to be just as enamored with her, and they quickly became a couple.

Alice proudly introduced Don to her family and friends, eager to incorporate him into her world. It wasn't long before she realized that she had neither met anybody in HIS life; nor had he given any indication that he had any intention of introducing her. When she brought it up, Don was a bit hesitant, explaining that his adult children were still grieving over their mother and that he didn't think that they were ready to accept the idea of him being with another woman. Alice understood at first, but after a while, she began to feel like a dirty little secret that he was hiding. Other things came to her attention. She noticed how, whenever they went out to dinner, it was always to some out of-the-way place where he wasn't likely to run into anybody he knew. Also, his late wife's photo was on his cell phone screen, and he was still wearing his wedding band. He continued to maintain strong ties to his late wife's relatives, often attending their family celebrations and other functions. Furthermore, Don would never call Alice or answer her calls if anybody else was around. Alice began to feel like she was sneaking around with a cheating husband. Every time she attempted to discuss the situation, Don complained that he felt "pressured," asking her to be patient and to give him more time to find a way to break the news to his children, relatives, and former in-laws.

Alice confided in me that she felt like Don's late wife would always be Number One and that he would never love her to that same degree. "I love him so much," she said. "He's everything I ever wanted in a man but it seems that he'll always belong to another woman, yet I'm not ready to give up on him. How can I make him understand how wonderful things can be for us? How long should I wait for him to be ready to bring our relationship out in the open?"

Ah, yes, it seemed too good to be true...the ugly truth finally came to light.

Now I'm no expert when it comes to relationships but I HAVE learned what NOT to do. As a rule, I will offer an opinion and some suggestions, but I won't try to force my ideas on anyone. Since Alice asked for my two cents, however, I was going to give her my honest opinion and it wouldn't be sugarcoated.

First of all, I told her, you can NOT "make him understand how wonderful things can be" for the two of you. He either recognizes the relationship potential or he doesn't. Secondly, it seemed to me that eight months after his late wife's death was far too soon for Don to have signed up on that dating site. After all, he had been married for twenty-six years to his high school sweetheart. He was at her bedside, holding her hand when she took her last breath. She was the only woman with whom he had ever been intimate. The problem, I said, was that Don did not know how to be alone. He was quite capable of taking care of himself physically, but he was just not EMOTIONALLY equipped to be single. Rita's death left a large void in his life that needed to be filled. His entire identity revolved around being her husband. He did not know who he was without her. Every part of his life was designed to his being part of a couple, and he desperately wanted to be back into a lifestyle that made sense again. Don was only looking to get HIS needs met without taking into consideration the effect that it would have on the unfortunate woman who was unknowingly drawn into a relationship with him.

Alice was angry. She felt duped, deceived, and humiliated, much the same way she felt when she was married to her womanizing ex-husband. Once again, she was involved with a man whose heart belonged to another woman. This time, however, the "other woman" was a deceased wife. At this point, Alice hated everything about Rita. She could no longer stand to hear even the mention of her name. She resented this unwelcome intruder whose spirit continued to get in the way of her happiness. One night, Don was at her house and they were watching a sitcom on television. In a wistful tone of voice, he said, "Rita LOVED this show. We used to watch it together all the time." (Don said *we*, meaning him and Rita). Alice finally snapped. She just couldn't take it anymore. "RITA, RITA, RITA! I am sick to death of hearing about that woman! She's gone! Accept it and get over her, will you? How would YOU like it if I kept bending YOUR ear about another man? Are you EVER going to get your head out of the past and start living in the present?"

Don was shocked and became equally angry. "WHAT THE HELL IS WRONG WITH YOU THAT YOU COULD BE SO JEALOUS OF A DEAD WOMAN? She was my WIFE, for God's sake! You can't just expect me to forget about somebody who was there for most of my adult life! You never had that kind of bond with another person so you can't understand what it's like!"

Alice tried to reason with him. "Don, I'm NOT jealous of her; I'm NOT asking you to forget about her. Maybe I have not been in your position, but you haven't been in mine either. How do you think it feels for ME to keep hearing you talk about how much you love and miss another woman? I was married to a man who always wanted somebody else and here I am again with a man whose mind is always on another woman. Don't you know how much that hurts? Are you EVER going to love ME that way, or am I once again wasting my time with a man who prefers to be with somebody else?"

Don reminded her that he "wasn't fully ready" to bring their relationship out in the open and asked her to be patient while he worked things out. "You have to remember," he argued, "I'm in foreign territory here. Rita is the only woman who has ever been a constant part of my life. We practically grew up together; we enjoyed many years in a comfortable, familiar routine that has been taken away from me, and I'm still trying to figure this out, to find out who I am now that she's gone. You really need to be more compassionate and understanding, Alice. You never struck me as a selfish, insensitive person, but this is exactly how you're acting!"

Alice lost it. "You're calling ME selfish and insensitive? You're getting everything YOU need out of this relationship. I provide you with companionship! Sex! Emotional support! What do I get?"

Don didn't miss a beat. "You seem to be enjoying the sex and companionship just as much as I am! I take you out to nice restaurants! I try to show you a good time whenever we're together, yet you're never satisfied. You just keep demanding more and more!"

"YOU CLUELESS SON-OF-A-BITCH!" she yelled. "Yes, you give me a lot — everything but your heart! You haven't even told anybody in your life about me, like I'm some shameful habit that you've been hiding! Yes, we go to nice restaurants, but they're always located in some out-of-the-way area where there's no chance of running into anybody you know."

"Have a little compassion," he said. "My kids are not over Rita's death either. My entire family loved her. And our friends miss her terribly. A lot of people are still grieving her death, yet you want me to bring you into the picture with a big smile on my face, parading you around like some kind of trophy! What you're asking me to do is to rub their noses in the fact that Rita is gone! How cold is THAT?"

Alice gave it right back to him. "Why should this be MY problem? If that's the way you feel, what the hell were you doing on a dating site? Why didn't you wait until you got over Rita before you tried to get involved with somebody else? It makes ME feel like a consolation prize! You should have remained alone until you got all this crap out of your system, but no, you were only thinking about what YOU needed and didn't stop to think twice before cluttering MY life with all this baggage!"

Alice and Don were obviously complete opposites in the way they saw this situation. It was a recipe for disaster.

Her anger finally spent, Alice's shoulders slumped in defeat as she finished venting. "How do I handle this?" she asked me.

I conceded that it was selfish of Don to drag another woman into his life when he obviously had not recovered from Rita's death. He was using her as a distraction from his pain. "Don't be his 'comfort woman'," I told her. "Otherwise, he'll become conditioned to seeing you as an emotional caretaker while he adjusts from being a husband to becoming a widower. Furthermore, after Rita died, Don was surrounded by the love and support of family and friends. Then he met you and never really had a chance to experience the full impact of being alone in this new life that had been forced upon him. He feels a sense of obligation to those who stood by him and helped him through it all. He may be afraid to disappoint those who loved Rita and still miss her. Your presence could be a painful indication that he's moving on and they may not be ready to face that."

"I can see that," Alice said.

"My advice is to back away," I said. "Don't spend as much time with Don. Get busy with your OWN family and friends. Become active in a local organization. Take a class. Get involved in some kind of hobby. Join a gym. Find a Meetup group. Do whatever you can to fill your time with things that are fun and rewarding. Surround yourself with people who will openly enjoy and appreciate YOU. The point is to stay occupied and happy on your own, apart from him. He's been with you long enough to have developed feelings for you, but he doesn't know what it's like not to have you around whenever he wants you. Give him a chance to miss YOU instead of Rita. You've made yourself available to him all the time. There's no challenge. No mystery. No incentive for him to chase after you. He cannot miss what he hasn't lost.

"Let him have a taste of being without you. Up until now, YOU have always been the one who has been wondering about the direction the relationship is headed. He needs to experience the discomfort and uncertainty of not knowing where HE stands for a change. I'm not suggesting that you break it off. I'm only saying that you need to set boundaries. You let him have all of you while he gave you only a portion of himself. By accepting this situation from the start, you gave him your silent approval of these conditions and taught him how to treat you. You cannot accept less than what you want, then keep seething inwardly because you're not getting everything you need. You'll never know what lengths he is willing to go to in order to make this work unless you take the risk of letting him go. Don't answer his calls and texts immediately. Wait a while before responding. Don't give him a minute-by-minute, detailed account of every move you make. Make sure that you remain upbeat and pleasant; if your actions display any trace of anger, they will lose all their power. You need to remain happy but busy. Act as if you're distant, distracted, and preoccupied. Trust me. If he cares enough about you, he'll notice the disconnection and he'll try to draw you closer again.

"You made an effort to discuss the situation with him and you tried to explain how it made you feel. He doesn't get it. All he did was become angry and defensive, accusing you of being jealous and insecure about a dead woman. That's a cop-out diversion tactic. He really doesn't understand how frustrating it is to be with somebody who is still attached to another person. You need to get your point across by your actions. That's the only way he'll ever take you seriously."

Alice sat quietly as I spoke, obviously trying to absorb this new approach. "But what if he just drifts away?"

"Well, then," I said, "if that's the case, then his feelings for you just aren't that strong and you need to accept that. Better to find out now than after you become any more emotionally invested in him. There's nothing more frustrating than trying to turn the wrong guy into the right one."

"But he's NOT the wrong guy! He's everything I ever wanted, if only he would stop looking back and pay attention to what's right in front of him!"

"Yes," I replied, "he's everything YOU ever wanted but are YOU everything HE ever wanted?"

"I could be," she argued, "if he would only give me a chance."

"Alice" I said, "he either wants you or he doesn't. The only way you'll know for sure is to let go. His reaction will tell you everything you need to know."

Naturally, it wasn't easy for Alice to take a step back and see less of Don; she felt like she was playing manipulative head games with him.

"It's NOT a game," I explained. "You're just setting boundaries and protecting yourself from a man who keeps you at a distance and hidden away from the most important people in his life."

That's when the light bulb went off in her head. She realized that HE was the one keeping HER at a distance; maybe it was time for her to do the same. He would never truly understand what it felt like to be wanting more than what he was getting unless he experienced it himself. Her life was an open book to him while a large part of HIS life was closed off to her. She realized that if she didn't take some kind of stand, things might never change. So she did just as I suggested and it made a huge difference!

It didn't take long before Alice got an opportunity to put her new plan into action. She had a group of close childhood friends who had often invited her to get together with them. She kept meaning to do so, but for some reason, she never got around to it. "Why not?" she finally asked herself, so she went ahead and made plans to go out with them. The following Friday night, she got together with these old friends for dinner and a few drinks. They laughed as they recalled the silly things they did as kids. They brought each other up to date about their marriages, relationships, jobs, children, health issues, etc. It felt great being with them again after all these years. She hadn't realized how much she missed her childhood friends. They had a wonderful time and at the end of the evening, they all promised each other that they would do it more often. She couldn't wait to see them again.

When she arrived back home after her evening out, Alice felt happier and more relaxed than she had in a long time. She hadn't realized how isolated she let herself get from everybody. She greatly enjoyed a wonderful meal with good friends and had a few glasses of wine with dinner, which filled her with a nice, mellow glow. It felt absolutely fantastic to be taking charge of her life. She started getting her life on track after she and her ex-husband split, but she had slipped back into old patterns of building her entire life around a man again after she met Don. For once, she was doing something proactive for herself instead of sitting around the house obsessing about her problems with Don or waiting for him to get away in order to spend time with her.

When she got settled back in at home after her night out with the girls, she saw that there were two missed calls from Don on her cell phone, a voicemail message ("Hi, Alice. I've been trying to reach you. I hope everything is okay."), and several text messages that he had sent while she was out.

Instead of getting back to him with a long, detailed commentary, she sent him a quick text, keeping it short and sweet. "Hi, Don. Got your messages. Sorry I didn't get back to you sooner. Going to bed now, it's late and I'm beat. Hope you had a good night. Talk soon! XXXOOO."

First thing the next morning, Don called. He was upset. "Where were you last night? I was worried sick! I tried to reach you several times and when I didn't hear from you, I thought something happened! Why didn't you call or at least send me a text sooner?"

Alice was smart. She didn't go into detail. "Geez, Don, I didn't mean to make you worry. I just lost track of the time."

"So where were you all that time?" he asked. "I called and sent text messages and it was nearly midnight before you got back to me! What were you doing out so late?"

Alice didn't miss a beat. "Don, you're overreacting. My phone was in my handbag and the ringer was off. I went out with some friends and we were having so much fun that I didn't realize how late it was." He wanted to know who she was with. "Nobody you know," she said. "Just some old friends I haven't seen in a while."

Alice COULD have been sarcastic and told Don that instead of wondering what SHE was doing, he could have spent that time reminiscing about Rita, but she resisted. She didn't want to sound spiteful or sarcastic because it would only anger him and initiate an ugly argument. Besides, if her actions had any trace of retaliation or anger, they would lose their effect. It wasn't about Alice ignoring Don, but rather, putting her focus back on herself where it belonged.

By putting herself ahead of him or their relationship, she sent Don the message that SHE considered herself to be important. Just because he didn't prioritize her enough to openly include her in every area of his life didn't mean that she was going to be waiting around to start living. She stopped trying to reason with him and let go. It was an empowering and effective move on her part.

That was only the beginning. Once Alice started to see how much her absence affected Don, it encouraged her to continue. She went to the salon and got herself a flattering new haircut. She started getting her nails done and spent a little extra time applying her makeup each day. She treated herself to some fashionable new clothes. She joined a gym and started going there on a regular basis. Alice wasn't in bad shape, but the exercise strengthened and toned her body. It felt great. She was surprised at how much more attractive she looked and how good it felt to pay extra attention to herself. She kept herself busy enhancing her quality of life. It also gave her a lift and a boost of confidence, which wasn't lost on Don. He appreciated her improved appearance and told her how nice she looked. She simply smiled and casually said "thank you."

As she continued to get progressively more involved in her own activities, Don became increasingly more concerned and somewhat clingy. He repeatedly wanted to know if they were okay or if they were drifting apart. "Don't be silly," she said with a light little laugh. "I've just been busy. You're making WAY too big a deal out of nothing. Spend some more quality time with your kids," she suggested. "I'm sure they'll appreciate your attention."

She quit complaining to Don about being hidden away from his family and friends; she finally realized that if he wanted to involve her in every part of his life, then he would do so without her having to ask. She wasn't going to beg. If the people in Don's life weren't ready to meet and accept her, then she didn't want to be around them either. There were too many others who liked and valued her company to push herself on those who didn't. It was that simple.

Alice also stopped inviting Don along when she spent time with her own family and friends. On a night that Don would normally be spending with his kids, he called Alice. "My daughter has a date and my son is going to a concert, so I'm on my own tonight. What do you say that we get together for a few hours?"

Alice later told me that she was enraged. "Why the hell does he let THEIR schedules dictate when and how much time we spend together?" she asked me.

"He will only get away with doing that if you allow it," I said.

Fortunately, Alice kept her cool. Instead of ripping into him, she sweetly said, "Don, I would have loved to see you tonight, but I already have plans. I'll tell you what, though. I am free tomorrow."

Don was dejected, explaining that his kids would be home the next day and he needed to be there for them.

"No worries; we'll just get together another time," she told him.

This was how it went for a while. Every time Don was free, Alice made sure she was busy; by the same token, she always managed to be free when she knew that HE was tied up with his kids or former in-laws. She turned the tables on him. She used to be the one complaining about wanting more out of the relationship; now it was HE who was upset because he wasn't getting enough time with HER. There really WAS something to be said about letting go. She gave HERSELF the time and attention she wanted from Don. She wasn't about to beg for any more than he was willing to give her, and at the same time, she stopped giving more than she was getting from him. He got a taste of what SHE had been feeling and he didn't much like it. As a result, he had a new appreciation for her, as well as a higher level of respect. Alice handled her problem beautifully.

It wasn't long before Don mentioned that he was thinking of bringing their relationship out in the open. Upon hearing that, she wanted to jump for joy, but instead, she casually said, "That's nice. By the way, did I mention that I signed up for an all-day group trip to the casino next weekend?"

Don was flabbergasted. After all, how many times did she tell him that she wanted to meet his family and friends? Now that he was finally willing to bring her around, she didn't appear to be all that excited over the prospect. Suddenly, it didn't seem to matter to her one way or the other anymore and he wanted to know why.

Once again, Alice kept her cool. "I realized that it wasn't that big a deal," she explained. "It's not necessary for me to meet the people in your life. You and I are happy and enjoying ourselves, and that's all that matters. I'm in a relationship with YOU — not your family and friends."

Don didn't like that one bit. She didn't seem to care as much; he felt her slipping away. He didn't want to go back to being alone, but he also needed to be sensitive to how it might affect his kids to see him with another woman after losing their mother. All this sneaking around, though, was taking a toll on his relationship with Alice. It seemed that no matter what he did, somebody was going to get hurt. Alice was right. He was putting everyone else's feelings ahead of his own. Maybe it was time for him to think about himself for a change. After all, his kids didn't stop dating or living THEIR lives. He, too, had a right to be happy.

Notice anything interesting here? Ever since Alice took back her power, Don's thoughts revolved more and more around HER instead of Rita. He also stopped wearing his wedding ring after she told him that it made her feel like she was seeing a married man. How easy was THAT? Yes, she did finally meet his kids, and although they didn't exactly welcome her with open arms, they weren't rude. She and Don also went out for dinner with several couples who had known Rita. It was a little awkward for them at first, seeing Don with Alice instead of Rita, but they were cordial and they made Alice feel like a welcome addition to their group.

This was the turning point in Alice's relationship with Don. They remained together, enjoying life as an exclusive couple. They're certainly not without problems, but they manage to work through them. They have jumped over many hurdles and it gets easier as time goes on.

This relationship could have taken a very different turn, had Alice continued trying to force the solution she wanted. Luckily, her story had a happy ending.

In the following chapters, I am going to discuss more of the most common obstacles and complaints that have plagued women whose partners are widowed.

4. WHAT'S IN A NAME?

How many times has your widowed partner called you by his late wife's name? That's what happened to Barbara. Her guy, Jim, slipped and called her "Connie," the name of his late wife. It was early on in the relationship, so she laughed it off. "You should have gotten into the habit of calling every woman 'Honey', this way, you'd NEVER get the name wrong," she joked. Jim laughed along with her and the moment passed.

It was only funny in the beginning, but after a while, she stopped laughing and let him know that it needed to stop. "MY NAME IS BARBARA!" she yelled.

"But it's just force of habit," he whined. "I've been with Connie for so long that it's second nature to me. I mean no disrespect to you. Don't make it out to be more than what it is. You're making too big a deal out of nothing."

Excuse me? Making too big a deal out of NOTHING? Since when did Barbara's feelings become 'nothing'?

Okay, let me play the devil's advocate here for a minute. Jim WAS married to Connie for many years. He spoke her name several times in the course of every day. It's a knee-jerk reaction. I totally get that. I also get what Barbara is saying.

Barbara is certainly justified for complaining when Jim accidentally calls her 'Connie'. When she confronts him about it, she's letting him know that it bothers her. She's speaking up as a matter of self-respect. Jim's point of view is equally valid. The problem is that Barbara's name is NOT 'Connie'. Jim could and should have handled his mistake with a little more sensitivity, instead of berating her and making her out to feel foolish for reacting the way she does.

A better response from him would be to say, "Oops! My bad! I apologize for calling you by Connie's name. I know it was thoughtless of me but it wasn't done deliberately. I'll do my best to be more careful not to do that from now on; if I do happen to slip up again, please try not to get too upset with me." I believe that had he responded that way, Barbara would have calmed down and a major conflict would have been prevented.

It's bad enough that Jim called her 'Connie', but by suggesting that Barbara was overreacting, he was being dismissive of her feelings, adding insult to injury. Nobody likes the implication that their thoughts and emotions are not valid. It's tantamount to saying that your feelings aren't important…that they don't count.

When Jim and Barbara first met, he loved to tell her all about Connie. At first, Barbara listened with interest and amusement. She thought it was endearing the way he spoke so highly of his late wife, but too much of anything is never good. Barbara began to feel like nothing more than a sounding board and wished that Jim would get his head out of the past and into the present with her. Barbara had high hopes for this relationship, but Jim's attitude when Barbara told him how it made her feel when he accidentally called her by his late wife's name is what sealed their Fate. For Barbara, it was the beginning of the end.

Barbara spent many years learning how to stand up for herself and to speak out when something didn't suit her. Jim's attitude was cavalier and indifferent. He neither took Barbara's concerns into consideration, nor did he assume any responsibility for his gaffes. Yes, it was an innocent mistake on his part, but he should have handled it with a little more understanding.

What should have been a minor issue turned out to be a deal breaker. No, Barbara didn't dump Jim for calling her 'Connie'. She stopped seeing him because of the way he responded when she told him about it. Her perception was that Jim didn't care enough about her feelings to even try to understand them. She believed that if he genuinely cared about her, he would have made it a point to take her feelings into consideration, even if he didn't agree with them. If this was any indication as to how he would handle future conflicts, Barbara decided that it would be better for her to back away from the relationship before she became more emotionally invested.

What's in a name? Not much, really. The problem in and of itself was not that Jim called Barbara by Connie's name. The problem was that Jim was incapable of stepping outside of himself to look at the situation from Barbara's point of view. He accused her of being overly emotional over something 'silly'. To her, it was an indication that he had no respect for her feelings.

Was Barbara wrong for ending the relationship? Not at all. She was only doing what she needed to do for herself. Her only other option would be to stay with him and suppress her feelings, rather than to risk his condemnation and criticism. Yes, she could have reminded herself that there were a lot of guys who did far worse things than this; she could have told herself not to be ridiculous, that she should count her blessings if this was the very worst complaint she had about Jim, but at what price? By holding everything inside, she would be seething with anger and resentment, which would poison the relationship in other ways. She was sparing them both a lot of heartache by quickly recognizing that their mindsets were too far apart to find a happy medium. That's what divorce attorneys like to refer to as "irreconcilable differences."

Feelings aren't facts. They are neither right nor wrong. They're an integral part of the package that makes a person who he or she is. People have a right to be themselves in their natural state. If one needs to hide behind a mask in order to gain approval and acceptance, they're not receiving unconditional love.

Relationships are challenging enough without having unresolved issues from the past contaminating them. This is particularly true of those dating a widower. Thanks to modern technology and social media, I have spoken at length with women from all over the world, different walks of life and varying economic backgrounds — women who are in love with widowers — and I am amazed at how similar their stories are.

Another one of the biggest pet peeves I have heard repeatedly when it comes to names is when a widower speaks of his late spouse by referring to her as his 'wife'. Okay, yes — she WAS his wife — but to speak of her that way in the present indicates that he still considers himself a married man. This is unsettling to his current girlfriend, fiancée, or wife. It's not just the widower who makes this mistake. Take Angie, for example. She accompanied her husband Tom, a former widower, to get an annual physical from his long-time family doctor.

The doctor smiled at Angie and said, "I've been treating Tom and his wife for many years."

Angie looked at the doctor and very politely but firmly corrected him, saying, "I'M his wife." Ouch!

So, yes, it's not only about slipping up and calling you by his late wife's name, but it's also the problem of keeping her in the present by referring to her as his "wife" instead of his LATE wife.

5. THE SHRINE

Charlie was in his forties when his wife Lisa died in a car accident. They had been married for eighteen years and were very happy together. They never had children; it was just the two of them. Charlie was, by nature, an outgoing, upbeat type of person who never had a bad day. After Lisa died, however, he went into a deep depression and started isolating himself.

His friends and family were worried about him and tried to raise his spirits. They urged him to make an effort to get out and take his mind off his grief. Finally, just to get everybody off his back, he agreed to join a bowling league with a couple of friends. He loved to bowl, and although he wasn't having a great time, he WAS enjoying himself a little bit. Eventually, he made friends with people on the other teams, taking special notice of a woman named Karen. She was friendly and appeared to be quite popular. She had a way of making people feel good when they were around her. He found himself paying closer attention to her and wanting to get to know her better. That proved to be more difficult than he thought. For one thing, Karen was very engaging and always had people around her. Secondly, he was a bit out of practice, not having dated for many years.

Finally, he saw an opening and struck up a conversation with her. Every week on bowling night, Charlie would search the place for Karen and made it a point to spend a little time talking with her. One day, he invited her to have coffee with him and she happily accepted. They talked for over an hour and he felt very comfortable with her, like they'd known each other forever. Karen listened sympathetically as Charlie told her all about Lisa. "She was the love of my life" he lamented.

Karen was in her thirties and had been engaged at one time but never married. "It didn't work out so we broke our engagement," she told Charlie.

Charlie was surprised to realize how much he looked forward to being with Karen. They started to see each other regularly over the next several months until they were together so much that Charlie finally asked Karen to move in with him. Karen was elated, thinking that she had finally found Mr. Right.

So she gave up her apartment and moved into Charlie's house, or, should I say, LISA'S house. Her clothes and shoes were still in the bedroom closet. Her cosmetics and personal items were in the bathroom. Karen saw traces of Lisa in every corner of the house. There was one room in particular that Karen found especially disturbing. It was a type of shrine. Every wall in that room told a story of Lisa's life with Charlie. There was a wedding photo of them hanging on the wall, along with a framed copy of their wedding invitation. There was a curio in the corner containing the ornament that topped their wedding cake, a small Lenox heart with their names and wedding date etched in gold, and various other sentimental items from many significant life events over the years. There was a book sitting on Lisa's desk with a bookmark to hold the page she was on just before she was in the accident that killed her. Inside the desk was an assortment of romantic cards that Charlie had sent to her over the years on Valentine's Day, her birthday, their anniversary, etc. Everywhere Karen looked, she saw Lisa. Worst of all, her ashes were there, sitting in a beautiful urn on the mantel. It felt like Lisa was going to walk in at any minute and demand to know why Karen was living in her house with her husband.

Karen felt like she had stepped into the life of Charlie's late wife, picking right up where Lisa left off. Charlie was baffled. "But it's just STUFF," he said. "Why do you let it get to you?"

"Because it's not MY stuff," Karen said. "This house belonged to another woman and it will never feel like MY home as long as Lisa's belongings and photos are out and observable everywhere." She told Charlie that this wasn't going to work for her, and that she couldn't live with Lisa in her face everywhere she looked. She was ready to walk out; better to lose HIM, she thought, than to lose HERSELF. Karen had no intention of staying in this mausoleum, and this is exactly what she told Charlie.

He loved Karen and honestly had never given this problem a second thought. He was utterly clueless, but now he was seeing the situation through HER eyes and realized that HE would not want to live in a house that still displayed traces of Karen's previous life with another man. They talked it over and decided to get a house of their own that held no history for either of them. They found a wonderful place in a different town and had a great time making it their own, a home that reflected a style that was unique to them as a couple. He boxed up all of Lisa's items and either disposed of them, donated them, or gave them to her relatives. Before he closed the door to his house for the last time, he spread Lisa's ashes around the outside of the property, then walked away to start a new life with a clean slate.

Today, Karen and Charlie are happily married with a baby on the way. This story could have had a very different ending. Charlie would have missed out on new, REAL love in his life and the family he always wanted had he continued hanging on to the memory of a woman who was no longer alive and would never be coming back.

6. HIS DISRESPECTFUL KIDS

Another one of the biggest and most common problems in relationships with widowers is their children. This includes the ones who have reached adulthood. Let's take Dave, for example. After his wife Maureen passed away, he felt a strong obligation to make it up to his kids for the loss of their mother and oh, did they milk it for all it was worth! His son and daughter were in their early twenties, but their father continued to coddle them as if they were children. They lived at home rent-free, did absolutely nothing around the house, and expected their father to cater to their every whim. Dave either didn't see what was happening or he looked the other way; whatever the reason, he jumped through unreasonable hoops for them.

Truthfully, his over-compensating wasn't a problem until he got involved with Julie, a woman he knew casually from the church that both he and his late wife had belonged to. Julie was divorced and had two kids of her own, both in college. Dave and Julie started going out to dinner, to the movies, and all the other usual things that couples do when they're dating. They had a great rapport and spent hours talking about everything under the sun. Dave told her all about Maureen's death. Julie shared the details of her painful divorce. The relationship was good and progressively developing into a serious one.

Dave decided it was time to have "the talk" with his kids about his intentions to make Julie a part of the family, and that's when all hell broke loose, to put it mildly.

His daughter flipped out. "How can you even THINK about being with anybody else, or moving a woman into our house so soon after losing Mom?"

Dave tried to reason with her. "Jennifer, your mother has been gone for over a year now. She was a wonderful woman and I was good to her. We were happy, but she's gone and nothing I do is ever going to change that. Julie is a great person and I think you'll like her."

Jennifer wanted no part of it. "Daddy, you can't mean that! I'll NEVER like Julie and why should I? She's never going to replace Mom!"

Dave's son Justin was even more outspoken. "This bitch jumped all over you before Mom was even cold in her grave and you fell for it! You can go out and get laid without moving her into OUR house. Man, talk about thinking with the wrong head!"

Dave became angry. "THAT'S ENOUGH, Justin! Don't you DARE talk about Julie that way! She's a good, hard-working mother who has two kids of her own. If the two of you would just give her a chance, you'll see what a nice person she is! I'm going to invite her out to dinner with the three of us and all I'm asking is for you to be polite to her."

Dave didn't tell Julie how badly things went with his kids. He figured that the kids were just thrown off balance by this unexpected turn of events and once they had a few days to get used to the idea, they'd calm down and be fine with it. He could not have been more wrong.

The following Saturday, Julie met up with Dave to have that dinner with him and his kids. They were rude, sullen, and sarcastic. They barely acknowledged Julie and directed all of their comments only to their father, effectively cutting Julie out of the conversation. "Dad, remember how much Mom loved this restaurant? I bet you like coming here because it reminds you of her."

On and on it went until Julie was fighting back tears. The evening was a disaster. Julie had serious doubts that the relationship would survive under the pressure of this hostility, but Dave waved her off. "They'll come around," he promised. "They're still grieving over their mother. They just miss Maureen so much. Please be patient and give them some time. I'll talk to them again. Everything will work out — you'll see." If only it was that simple.

Julie, too, had "the talk" with her own children, but it was a very different scenario. Frankie, her son, was the first to speak up. "Mom, Morgan and I were hoping that you'd find a nice guy. You deserve to be happy. Your whole life has revolved around the two of us since you and Dad divorced. Dad and Donna have a good life together and it's about time that YOU found somebody special."

Morgan, her daughter, concurred. "Dave sounds like a good guy, Mom. Go for it!"

The relationship between Dave and Julie continued to thrive until they moved in together. They agreed that it was more logical to live in Dave's much larger house. Each of the kids would have their own room and it would be financially easier for them all to live under one roof instead of supporting two separate households. Dave and Julie looked forward to blending their families with high hopes that all would be well. It wasn't.

Jennifer and Justin hated the situation. They resented these intruders who took over their home, particularly Julie who "stole" their mother's life. Julie did her best to make friends with them. She cooked meals that she thought they'd enjoy and bit her tongue whenever they were nasty to her, which was all of the time. They would bring junk food and take-out home, leaving trash and dirty dishes all over the place and would refuse to eat anything that Julie prepared. "This tastes like garbage. Mom spoiled Dad with her delicious meals. You'll kill him with YOUR cooking." That wasn't all, either. They were sloppy, throwing dirty clothes all over the floor and making a big mess after Julie had worked hard to keep the house clean.

She complained to Dave but he only got defensive. "Didn't I ask you to give them some time? They'll adjust, but it won't happen overnight. You have to give them a chance to get used to this. They have already had so many changes in their young lives; they're just having trouble dealing with so many things at once. Their mother died and they're still grieving. Try to have some compassion."

"But Dave, MY kids have been through a lot, too. They had to deal with their father and me going through a divorce; they had to get used to the idea of their dad getting married again to somebody else. They're both in college and working part-time, which isn't easy. To top it off, they were uprooted when we all moved into your house. If that's not bad enough, YOUR kids treat us all like trespassers. This doesn't feel like home and my kids are walking around the house on eggshells. Just the same, they're careful not to disrupt or disturb your kids, they pick up after themselves and they're always polite to you. YOUR kids don't go to school and they don't work. They make a huge mess, they don't lift a finger to help out and they don't contribute a dime. This house doesn't feel like home to my kids, yet you don't see THEM acting like spoiled, selfish, entitled brats!"

Dave didn't agree. "Don't you think you're being a little harsh? Your kids still have a mother AND a father, plus a stepmother who loves them. MY kids only have ME."

"That's THEIR choice, Dave. They have me, too, if they would just accept me," Julie argued.

It was a losing battle.

It was bad enough living in this war zone with this very different set of kids. Frankie and Morgan were angry that there seemed to be two sets of rules. They were expected to be patient and understanding while Jennifer and Justin had a free pass to do whatever they wanted, whenever they wanted. Dave's kids got away with murder. They loved keeping Julie and her kids on edge. Jennifer would go into Morgan's room and "borrow" things that weren't returned, often misplacing them. She once "accidentally" spilled red nail polish all over Morgan's favorite blouse.

Morgan would complain, only to be told to stop "accusing" Jennifer of doing all these things on purpose without any proof. Justin did the same to Frankie, often messing around on his computer and erasing files.

Everything came to a head, and Julie finally snapped. "They need to have boundaries, Dave! Your kids have absolutely NO rules to follow! How is this situation ever going to get better if you continue to make excuses for your kids? They're turning into monsters, and they're completely out of control. You can't possibly be so blind that you can't see what's going on right under your nose! It has become intolerable, yet you do nothing to stop your kids from torturing all of us. We are made to feel unwanted and unwelcome here. We can't take much more of this. If your kids are trying to destroy us, they're doing a good job of it. I just hope you straighten them out before it's too late!"

Dave promised that he'd "talk to them" and that things would change. The only thing that changed was that his kids put on a good face whenever their father was around and were as vicious as ever toward Julie, Frankie, and Morgan when Dave wasn't there to see it. He tried to smooth things over, but Justin and Jennifer played the grief card, accusing Dave of being happier without their mother every time he tried to crack down on them. They knew how to use guilt to their advantage. I have to give Julie a lot of credit. She stuck it out far longer than most women would have, myself included. She continued trying to get Dave to see the light. "What will become of your kids if something happens to you? Do you think the rest of the world will coddle them because they lost their mother? You're over-compensating; they have no coping skills. They believe that the world owes them something because their mother died. Believe me, Dave, you're only hurting them in the long run because they are being conditioned to think that what they're doing is okay. You're setting them up for a rude awakening one day. Why can't you understand that?"

As always, Dave swore that he would resolve the problem, but when push came to shove, he always caved in to his kids.

Julie had had enough. She couldn't take it anymore. She, too, felt a sense of guilt for what this was doing to HER kids, so she packed them up and moved out; it was the only way they'd have any peace of mind. She rented a small, modest house in a working-class neighborhood, which was a major step down from Dave's big, fancy house in a more affluent area, but at least it was theirs. They were able to live in peace, without any tension and hostility. Julie handled the breakup beautifully. She held her head up, kept her dignity intact, resisted the urge to tell his kids off, and left Dave on friendly terms. Later, her tears would flow in the privacy of her new home. She loved Dave and she was devastated that it didn't work out. She didn't regret her relationship with him, though. He taught her that she could love and be loved again. They would have made an ideal couple. It was his kids who ruined it.

Julie was now much more discerning than she was before she got involved with Dave. This experience taught her to guard her heart until she knew it was safe. She was especially wary of widowers. A few years went by and she eventually met the man whom she would later marry. Bob was a strong but gentle guy with an appreciation for Julie's quiet strength, and he had respect for her boundaries. He was patient as he waited to earn her trust; his efforts paid off when she accepted his proposal. She still runs into Dave from time to time at the church and always takes a few minutes to exchange pleasant conversation with him. He continues to date and admits to having several failed relationship attempts since Julie left him. He now expresses regret for having let her get away, conceding that he should have taken a more aggressive stand with his kids who, to this day, continue to destroy his relationships. He made a huge mistake by letting them get away with what they were doing and he paid — and continues to pay — dearly for it.

Julie's story had a much happier ending and rightfully so because she hung in there and did her best to make it work. But ultimately, she couldn't make Dave see what he didn't want to face. To this day, Dave hasn't had any luck finding lasting love. Julie and Bob, on the other hand, are enjoying married life and couldn't be happier.

Kids can be very destructive. They should never, EVER be permitted to wield that kind of power over their parents. What you permit, you promote. Yes, I understand that they lost their mother, but that does not give them license to take it out on the rest of the world. As for the widowed father of these children, as much as he would love to offset his kids' pain over losing their mother, the fact is that they are going to be hit with curveballs from time to time. They should not be shielded from the harsh realities of life. It's nobody's fault that they're hurting and it's not the surviving parent's responsibility to spare them the opportunity to develop strength and coping skills. They cannot be given a permanent set of training wheels, preventing them from learning how to ride a bike. As hard as it may be, they have to experience failures and scraped knees before they can learn to balance themselves without a crutch.

The widower is not doing his kids any favors when he allows them to dictate to him.

All they're learning is how to manipulate him. Does the widower secretly worry about losing his kids if he doesn't give in to their every whim? If so, trust me when I tell you that they can sense fear and they WILL play their father like a harp. They will never love and respect him for being too easy on them. They'll just learn that he is someone to be used for their own selfish convenience and they will fight tooth and nail to keep him mired in guilt and a false sense of responsibility in order to continue getting whatever they want. They will neither respect nor value their father as a person. They're being encouraged to abuse and manipulate their father, and to have no regard for his feelings, wants, and needs. By allowing his kids to get away with this kind of behavior, he is ruining any chances for them (and for you) to live a happy, fulfilling life. It's cruel to be kind. It's better for the children to cry now than for the parents to cry later.

7. MINI-WIFE

Some widowers have children, particularly daughters, who assume the role of the deceased spouse. This is called "mini-wife syndrome." The main characteristics of this condition are:

1. A female child who feels entitled to the complete and total attention of her father.
2. Strong objections to the new woman in her father's life.
3. Competes with the woman in her father's life for his attention.
4. Demands evidence that she is #1 in her father's eyes.
5. Attention seeking behavior, especially from that of her father.
6. Becomes incapable of her own relationships due to unrealistic expectations.

Mike is a perfect example of a man with a "mini-wife." He and his late wife Joan enjoyed a happy marriage. They had only one child, a daughter named Lindsay. She had a very warm and close relationship with her parents, Mike and Joan. Lindsay was twenty-eight when Joan passed away after a long, painful illness and Lindsay was devastated; her world was shattered. Joan's death was inevitable, but Lindsay was in denial, believing that her mother would recover. After Joan died, Lindsay desperately wanted to keep everything as normal as possible, so she assumed the role of her father's "mini-wife," taking over all of the household chores that Joan used to do. Lindsay knew all of Joan's recipes and when Mike came home from work, he and Lindsay had dinner together as usual. Lindsay was determined to keep their lives as close as possible to the way they were when her mother was alive. This behavior in the daughters of widowers is referred to as "mini-wife behavior." The daughters do this to keep their widowed fathers content, in order to minimize his need and desire to bring a new woman into the fold. They take on the role of their father's wife and resent it when their father gives his attentions to another woman. It is emotional incest. To a daughter, it's unthinkable that her father is a healthy, red-blooded male who still has physical and emotional needs that can only be satisfied in a romantic relationship with another adult. Lindsay couldn't bear to think of her father that way.

Mike was realistic. He had no misgivings about moving on. He was an excellent husband to Joan and remained so until they were parted in death. His obligation to this marriage was finished. He understood the uncertainty of life and the fact that bad things can and do happen. He realized that life was short and unpredictable and that there was nothing to be gained by prolonged grieving. Unlike his daughter, he was resigned to the fact that Joan's death was coming, so when it finally happened, he held up well. Still, it didn't stop him from falling into an occasional funk. The truth was that he didn't know who he was without his late wife. His very identity revolved around being Joan's husband. He knew he had to let go of what no longer existed in order to start a new life. He wanted to be happy again. He deserved it. The problem was that he didn't have a clue as to how to go about it.

Mike and Joan had married at a young age and neither of them had any real dating experience with others. They only knew each other, so after Joan died, Mike felt that half of him was gone. He wondered what would become of his life. He was thinking of all the empty years that stretched ahead and dreaded the thought of spending the rest of his life alone. In spite of his attempts to remain optimistic, he became despondent. He was no longer a member of the couples' world, but he couldn't see himself fitting into the singles' scene either.

He confided in his close friend, Joe. "I don't know how to deal with this," he complained. Joe suggested counseling. "Counseling for WHAT? There are no counselors in the world who can fast-forward me through this process. How could they possibly understand what I'm going through unless they lived through this same situation themselves? It's easy for a counselor to tell me what to do, but how can they justify giving advice that they never had to follow themselves?"

Joe urged him to keep an open mind. "Listen, Mike. I know of a great therapist who helped a neighbor of mine who went through the same thing. Let me give you her number. Go for one or two sessions before you decide that it won't help."

That's how Mike ended up going for counseling. He was pleasantly surprised to discover what a relief it was to be able to vent his frustrations to a professional who listened to him intently and let him get it all out without interrupting. After he was finished, the therapist gently asked him how he felt about the idea of dating again.

"How could I go about finding a woman to take out on a date? I'm over fifty. The only women I know are those whom I've known for years, such as Joan's friends, my co-workers, or the women who are married to my buddies. I'm not into the nightclub scene. I wouldn't even know where to start!"

"Have you ever considered online dating sites for older singles?" asked the therapist. Mike told her that he wasn't very computer literate. "Perhaps you have a tech-savvy friend who could help you out," she suggested.

That was how Mike found himself taking his first dip into the dating pool and what an experience it was! Joan had been deceased for about two years at this point. Mike went out with several women but none whom he desired to date a second time. There was June, a loud, aggressive, divorcee; Sandy, a provocative flirt who was all over him; Linda, a needy, insecure woman who was desperately seeking approval and validation; Sue, a heavy drinker who was already tipsy at the beginning of their date; Nancy, a widow who was eager to get married again; Fay, an independent professional who bored him with details of her many impressive accomplishments; and then there was Joanne who was looking for somebody to take care of her. All the women had one thing in common: they were jaded in some way. Mike couldn't see himself being with any of them, and he began to lose hope of ever finding a decent, well-balanced woman in his own age bracket.

Finally, he met Darlene, who seemed to have great potential. She was attractive, pleasant, fun to be with, and independent without coming off as arrogant. Mike liked her a lot. After several dates, he mustered up the courage to tell her that his feelings for her were strong — so much so that he lost all interest in dating anyone else. He even admitted that he took down his dating profile and asked Darlene if she would consider an exclusive relationship with him. She would and she did.

He dropped Darlene off after a date one evening, went home, and happily told his daughter that he had met a really nice woman who had serious future potential.

To his surprise and disappointment, Lindsay's eyes filled with tears. She couldn't imagine her father being with anyone but her mother. "Dad, why can't it just be the two of us? We're doing okay, aren't we? The house is clean, I take care of the laundry and we have dinner together every night like we always did. The only thing missing is Mom and we don't need anybody else to take her place."

Mike tried to make Lindsay understand. "Someday you're going to want to get married and have a family of your own and then where will that leave me? I loved your mother, but she's gone, Lindsay. I'm lonely for companionship. I love that we're so close, but you're my daughter. I don't want you to feel responsible for me. You should be out having fun with your friends, not here all the time, taking care of the house and me. We both deserve to be happy and enjoy life."

Lindsay said nothing, but she was visibly shaken by this new development. Mike was sure that in time she would change her mind.

A few months later, Mike brought Darlene home to meet his daughter. Lindsay gave Darlene a disinterested, obligatory "hello" and immediately turned her attention back to the magazine she was reading.

This is the way it went whenever Darlene was in Mike's house. Lindsay was sullen, acted as if Darlene was invisible, and didn't even acknowledge her presence; she simply spoke with her father as if the two of them were alone. "Dad, I washed and folded your clothes; they're in your drawer and, by the way, dinner will be ready at six o'clock."

Without actually saying so, Lindsay was marking her turf, letting Darlene know that she wasn't welcome, needed, or wanted. That wasn't all. Lindsay went out of her way to make Darlene feel uncomfortable, although she was subtle about it. One time when Darlene was at the house with Mike, Lindsay said, "Dad, remember that great vacation we had with Mom in the Bahamas? Well, I found a photo of the three of us that was taken during that trip. I had it enlarged, framed, and got two copies made. I put one of them on the nightstand next to your side of the bed."

Lindsay took advantage of every opportunity to make Darlene feel like a trespasser. Although Mike wasn't oblivious to his daughter's rude behavior, he dismissed Darlene's concerns. "She's just having a hard time adjusting to her mother's death. Be patient and give her some time. She'll come around."

Hmm…isn't this exactly what Dave said to Julie about HIS kids? Famous last words. Same story with different characters.

Darlene confided in me. "I've done everything I can think of to bond with Lindsay, but she wants nothing to do with me. I'm in love with Mike. We're so good together, but I'm afraid his daughter is going to screw it up for us. God forbid…Daddy has a girlfriend — what a NIGHTMARE! It's not MY fault her mother died. I can't continue feeling guilty because Mike loves me. I'm not doing anything wrong, and I've never been anything but nice to her, yet she acts like I'm some kind of home-wrecker. How can I turn this around?"

My advice to Darlene was to stop trying to bond with Lindsay. "You can't make her see what she doesn't want to face. You're fighting a losing battle. My philosophy is that I don't want anyone who doesn't want me. I make it a point to surround myself with people who like me and appreciate my company. I don't waste my time or energy trying to gain the acceptance and approval of those who clearly don't want to be bothered with me," I told her.

"But won't that cause problems between Mike and me?" Darlene asked.

I explained to her that Lindsay was the one who set the tone. If Mike should accuse her of being rude, I advised her to explain to him that she's just giving Lindsay space. "She made it clear that she doesn't want to be bothered with you. Just tell Mike that you don't want to force yourself on his daughter. He can't possibly argue with THAT." I also advised her to limit her time at Mike's house and to minimize all possible exposure to Lindsay. "She knows that you're jumping through hoops to win her over, and you're giving her the opportunity and satisfaction of being able to reject you again and again. If you allow her to become a cause for contention between you and Mike, her 'divide and conquer' tactics will succeed. Don't give her that kind of control. Indifference is powerful; she'll learn that she cannot shake or rattle you. Once she sees that you can take her or leave her and that she can't destroy your relationship with her father, you'll put HER in the position of being the one left out in the cold. Give this approach a try."

Darlene understood what I was saying. She made it a habit to spend time with Mike at HER house instead of his. She stopped asking him to invite Lindsay along on some of their outings, and on the rare occasions when she was in Lindsay's company, she didn't go out of her way to make conversation. In other words, she gave Lindsay a dose of her own medicine.

Mike noticed and didn't like it. "Why are you being so cold toward my daughter?" he demanded to know.

Darlene was taken aback. "Excuse me? I have made several attempts to have a conversation with her. All I get are one word answers. How many times do you expect me to try to interact with someone who clearly wants nothing to do with me?"

Mike disagreed. "You're playing tit for tat," he argued.

"No, I'm not," Darlene shot back. "Lindsay doesn't want to be bothered with me and you damn well know it. I'm not going to push myself on her. That will only make her despise me that much more. If she wants to be friendly with me, I'm here, but I won't force myself on someone who doesn't want me. I DO have SOME self-respect and besides, it hurts that she can't see any good in me. I haven't done anything to deserve her attitude and behavior toward me."

Mike couldn't argue with that.

Mike and Darlene's relationship continued to blossom and they fell more and more in love. They couldn't get enough of each other. They took nice vacations, went out for dinner, went to the movies, enjoyed occasional weekend getaways, and it became common for Mike to sleep over at Darlene's house at least three nights a week. Sometimes they watched a movie; other times, they each did their own separate thing, enjoying a comfortable silence, happy just to be together. This is the way things went for several months.

One night, Mike called Darlene, saying that he had returned home from work that day to find his daughter crying. "Apparently, Lindsay was upset at being alone in the house so much since I've been involved with you. It was bad enough that her mother died; now I'M gone most of the time. She says she feels like she lost BOTH parents."

Mike was torn.

Darlene saw right through Lindsay's manipulation tactic and wasn't about to get sucked into it. "Well, then, I think you should spend more time at home with Lindsay," she told Mike. "She needs you. Maybe we should see less of each other until she feels better about us."

Mike was relieved but concerned. "Are you sure that won't cause any trouble between us?" he asked Darlene.

"Not at all," she replied. "It's not a problem. Don't worry about me. This will give me time to catch up on some things that I've been neglecting."

I gave Darlene the thumbs up, telling her that she handled this situation beautifully. "Make it difficult for him to get in touch with you," I advised her. He can't argue because you're giving him more time with his daughter. You're taking one for the team."

So, Darlene did as I suggested. She went out with her friends, did some shopping, got involved with some local community activities, and signed up to take a class. Mike called her constantly, hoping to make plans to see her. More often than not, Darlene didn't answer the phone and he ended up talking to her voicemail or sending her text messages that weren't returned until later.

Mike got worried. "You're never home anymore, and I can never seem to reach you. I feel like we're drifting apart."

Darlene laughed it off. "Don't be silly! I'm just keeping busy so that I don't go stir crazy. I get bored sitting around the house. Why don't you and Lindsay go somewhere and do something fun? It might do her some good to get out of the house! You need to be there for Lindsay, Mike. God knows that I don't want to give her any more reason to resent me. I don't want her to feel like you've abandoned her."

Oh, yes…Darlene was as cool as a cucumber. She played it well.

Unsurprisingly, Mike unleashed his frustrations on to Lindsay. "Why don't you get out and spend more time with your friends? It's not fair that you want to just mope around this house all the time and expect me to hang around here with you. I have feelings, too. You're not the only one who lost somebody. Your mother's death hurt me just as much as it did you. You're so wrapped up in your own misery that you don't even stop to think about anyone else. You won't try to get to know Darlene. You won't even give her a chance! She has invited you to join us several times, but you always refuse. Don't you think you're being a bit selfish? You need to get on with your life."

When Lindsay started crying again, Mike softened, but just a bit. "Here's what I'll do. Pick three nights each week and I'll spend them with you. We'll do whatever you want. The rest of the week is mine. I want to be with Darlene. I don't want to lose her over this. She's been more than patient and has offered to step aside out of consideration for YOU. She has a lot of compassion for you even though you treat her like dirt! You better snap the hell out of it because if I'm forced to make a choice, you may not like it!"

Do you see what happened here? Lindsay played the guilt and manipulation card in an effort to drive a wedge between Mike and Darlene and it came back to bite her in the end. Give people what they think they want. Never try to compete. Blood is always thicker than water and you will appear to be insecure, possessive, and insensitive if you try to break that bond. Instead of arguing with Mike, insisting on her own way, and demanding that he set boundaries with Lindsay, Darlene stepped aside and handed Mike back to his daughter on a silver platter. She then made herself VERY scarce. Lindsay fought tooth and nail to keep Mike and Darlene apart, but she lost. Darlene was clever. She graciously took the high road by backing away and this gave Mike and Lindsay time to sort things out themselves. Instead of arguing with Mike and competing with his daughter for his time and attention, she gave Lindsay exactly what she wanted. Darlene was too wise to sit around hoping Mike would call or to make demands that he spend more time with her. Darlene was the bigger person, offering to sacrifice the relationship for the sake of his daughter and all this did was make Lindsay look petty, demanding and selfish by comparison. Mike felt Darlene slipping away from him and blamed Lindsay. This is a great lesson for ANY relationship situation. You will lose anyone you try to hold too tightly. This is not easy to do but you will come out ahead when you sacrifice momentary relief for long term satisfaction. Better to forfeit a few battle victories in order to win the war.

In the end, Mike set Lindsay straight of his own free will. It also opened his eyes to the reality of the situation. He couldn't blame Darlene for any part of this problem. She willingly gave up her time with him so he could be with Lindsay instead of kicking up a fuss and putting him in the middle. She just went about her business, going out and enjoying herself, giving Mike plenty of time and freedom to be with his daughter. The best and most important part of all was that Mike got a taste of what it felt like not to have Darlene around. She gave him a chance to miss her, and he didn't like it one bit.

As a rule, it's never a good idea to push a man into doing anything or to issue an ultimatum. He'll only go in the opposite direction. Give him the freedom and the dignity to make his own choices, then respond accordingly, like the way Darlene did. She didn't threaten to end it if Mike didn't straighten out his daughter. She let her actions speak for her. Darlene let Mike decide what to do about Lindsay; he had every right to spend all of his spare time with his daughter but he had to take what came with it, which was the risk of letting Darlene slip out of his life. Darlene didn't make demands, but she wouldn't allow Mike to have it both ways. Guess who won this battle? Mike and Darlene are happily married now.

Do you think this is where their story ends? Oh, it gets BETTER. You're going to LOVE the way the rest of this situation unfolds. Talk about karma! The next chapter is a real humdinger. Get out the popcorn and curl up in a comfy spot…you're in for a treat!

8. TIME WOUNDS ALL HEELS

Let's face it…nothing ever stays the same. Time is a great equalizer; it changes dynamics and circumstances in spite of what we do. It levels the playing field if you wait long enough to let time work its magic. And there's nothing we love more than to see our abusers get what's coming to them.

The last chapter was about the problems Darlene experienced with Mike's mini-wife daughter, Lindsay. Mike and Darlene got married and Darlene moved into Mike's house. Lindsay was thirty-one years old by this time. She was never completely comfortable with Darlene. Their relationship was no longer strained, but it wasn't warm and fuzzy either. Lindsay only tolerated Darlene and wasn't home with Mike and Darlene very much. When she wasn't working, she was out with her friends or on a date. One by one, her friends were getting married and having babies. Lindsay, too, was eager to find a nice guy, get married and have a house and family of her own.

About two years later, while at the wedding reception of a friend, Lindsay met a really nice guy. Paul was the cousin of the groom and he asked Lindsay to dance. They hit it off beautifully, and by the end of the night, they had plans to see each other again. At forty-five, Paul was twelve years older than Lindsay. He was a solid, stable man with a successful contracting business. He had been previously married. He was the father of three teenagers…and he was also a widower.

Lindsay and Paul fell deeply in love. They got married and Lindsay moved into the house that he lived in with his late wife. I won't get into specifics here. To make a long story short, Paul's kids hated Lindsay and wanted no part of her. They didn't even try to hide the bitter resentment they felt toward her. This was their MOTHER'S house and they never let Lindsay forget that. They took down the wedding photo of her and Paul, replacing it with the wedding photo of Paul and their late mother. Lindsay's clothes and other personal belongings mysteriously ended up missing or damaged. The kids were hostile, rude, and downright nasty. Paul's kids made Lindsay's life a living hell.

To make matters worse, Paul looked the other way. His kids missed their mother terribly and he constantly made excuses for their behavior. He gave Lindsay absolutely no support. Lindsay was beside herself, and she knew of only one other person who experienced and understood what she was going through: her father's wife, Darlene. Lindsay desperately wanted to confide in her, but she was afraid that Darlene would rub her nose in it, by saying, "What goes around, comes around." For a while, she suffered in silence until she couldn't take it any longer.

Lindsay finally stopped by the house to see Darlene when she knew her father wasn't home. "I'm so sorry for the way I treated you. How did you put up with me? What should I do about Paul?" Lindsay wailed.

Darlene would have LOVED to say, "Welcome to MY world," but she resisted. This was her chance to bond with her husband's daughter.

Darlene gave Lindsay the same advice I gave her a few years earlier. "Come and stay with us for a while," Darlene suggested. Let Paul deal with his kids by himself. Give him a chance to miss you."

Lindsay was skeptical. "Won't that be the same thing as rewarding those brats for the way they've been treating me? They WANT me out of their house. I hate to give them the satisfaction of leaving. I'll only be letting them know that their nasty actions were successful!"

Darlene disagreed. "If you remember, Lindsay, I had the same problem with you when I was dating your father. Your father saw you crying; he was torn between wanting to be with me and wanting to ease your pain, so I made it easy for him. I offered to step out of the picture, and you remember how it played out. Your father missed me so much that he took the necessary steps to straighten the problem out. If I had tried to compete with you for your father, things might have turned out very differently. Lindsay, you're the adult here. Take the high road and let Paul experience the full impact of living without you. He's happy now and he has grown comfortable with you. He loves you and he won't give you up that easily, but you have to give him a chance to realize what he could lose. This will always be your home and I'd love for you to stay here for as long as you need to. Tell Paul that you're going to stay with us for a while until his kids feel better about you and watch how it unfolds. One more thing…don't badmouth his kids; it'll only work against you."

Later that day, Paul came home to find Lindsay packing. "What's going on?" he asked.

Lindsay stayed calm. "I love you so much, Paul, but I can't build my happiness on someone else's misery. Your kids don't accept me. They don't want me here. We both know that. The situation isn't getting any better.

This house doesn't feel like home to me. Everywhere I turn, there are reminders of your late wife. The kids won't even let me keep a photo of myself anywhere. My belongings are either being damaged or they end up missing. Don't get me wrong…I'm not accusing anyone of anything. Maybe it's me. I'm so stressed out that I might be misplacing things without realizing it. This is a bad situation. The kids are not happy. I'm not happy, and I feel their resentment. I'm not myself anymore. I hate the way I feel all the time. I understand what your kids are going through because MY father remarried after my own mother died. I was an adult when it happened, but I still had a hard time with it. It's not my fault that your kids lost their mother, but I'm tired of getting the brunt of their pain and anger. Maybe we all need some time apart to figure things out. I'm not leaving you, but I DO need a break from the constant tension and hostility here. Take the kids out. Do fun things with them. They need some quality time with you by themselves. I don't want to be the one standing in the way of their happiness."

Paul was upset. "Lindsay, they're just kids. You know how teenagers are. They can't be THAT bad."

"They ARE that bad, Paul. You don't see what goes on when you're not around. The only crime I committed was falling in love with you. I don't deserve to be crucified for that. Look, I'm not walking out on you. I'm just giving your kids some time to have you all to themselves. I'll be staying with Dad and Darlene."

After Lindsay left, Paul was depressed. His kids, on the other hand, were visibly elated. They didn't notice or seem to care that their father was utterly miserable. They went right back to their after-school activities or hanging out with their friends. After a few days, Paul became angry and sat them down. "Listen, guys…you wanted Lindsay out of here. Now she's gone. You got what you wanted. I'm here all by myself most of the time with no one to talk to, while you're all off having fun with your friends and going about your usual routine. So here's the deal: If things have to be this way in order for you to be happy, fine, but you all have to do your part. Starting today, you will have to take turns cleaning, doing the laundry, and getting dinner ready. You will also have to stay home and keep me company every evening after work. If it's going to be just us, so be it, but I'm not going to be the only one who suffers the consequences."

Paul called Lindsay on her cell phone to tell her what was going on, but she didn't answer. He then tried calling the house and Darlene answered. "Lindsay's not here, Paul. I think she went out with a few of her friends. She didn't say when she'd be back. To be honest, I haven't seen much of her lately, but the next time I do, I'll let her know you called." Darlene had Lindsay's back all the way.

Paul's mind started racing. *Why is Lindsay out so much? Is she seeing someone else? Is she happier without me? Does she still love me? Were the kids so bad that they drove her away for good? Will she ever come back?* His thoughts went on that way until he couldn't take it anymore. He went over to Mike and Darlene's, determined not to leave until he had a chance to talk to Lindsay. Luckily, she was there. They went out for coffee in order to talk privately.

"Paul, I can't live in that house. I can never forget that it belonged to another woman first. It'll never really feel like my own home. Whenever I try to change anything, it makes the kids feel like I'm wiping out all traces of their mother. I love you but I can't deal with this. I think we should buy another house — a place we can make a home of our own. I want OUR wedding photo on the wall, not the wedding photo of you and your late wife. I want the house to be only a reflection of US. If the kids want photos or other visible reminders of their mother, they'll have to keep them in their rooms. I want my OWN furniture, appliances, and dishes. I don't want to sleep in HER bed anymore. We have a decent income with our combined salaries, and I'll have the right to do what I want in a house that belongs to me. Furthermore, you need to set some ground rules with the kids. It's the only way. They don't have to like me, but they have to respect me; otherwise, it'll never work."

Paul was willing to accept Lindsay's conditions. She never went back to his house. She stayed with Mike and Darlene until she and Paul bought a house of their own. True to his word, Paul kept his kids in line. I can't say that their lives became a fairy tale, but it was tolerable.

Just as Lindsay's father did with Darlene, Paul was willing to do whatever was necessary to keep his marriage to Lindsay together. The most wonderful part of all is that Lindsay grew to love and respect Darlene, having benefitted from her patience and wisdom. Darlene's advice and support helped to save Lindsay's marriage. On Darlene's most recent birthday, Lindsay bought a birthday card for a "Stepmother" and inside she wrote: "Happy Birthday to my Second Mother. My father could not have picked a better woman than you. I love you. Your devoted stepdaughter, Lindsay."

Darlene broke down and cried. Never in a million years did she expect this from Lindsay. To this day, they have a warm and loving relationship.

9. THE WIDOWER'S HALO

Some widowers love playing the grief card. They thrive on all the sympathy and attention they continue to get, even long after the death of their wife. They fancy themselves to be some kind of saint who manages to struggle through life, even though their hearts have been ripped out. Even when he's dating or involved with another woman, the perception is that the widower is simply "going through the motions," earning himself even more respect and admiration for putting one foot in front of the other, trying to go on in spite of his sadness. Ah, yes, they just LOVE wearing that widower's halo.

Said one woman married to a former widower, "I feel like I'm nothing more than a time filler, getting only the leftover crumbs after he gave his life wholeheartedly to his late wife. It's as if he's only giving me the bare minimum necessary to maintain our marriage when I know this wasn't the case with his late wife and, quite frankly, I'm tired of it all."

If you're a woman involved with a man who exploits his widowed status, you have a sizeable problem. These guys don't want to let go of their martyrdom; yet they don't want the loneliness and other disadvantages that come with being widowed. They get involved with another woman, expecting her to be okay with it while they openly carry a torch for their late wives. The people in this man's life are gentle and indulgent with him, as he struggles to find happiness in a new relationship.

Take Bob, for example. He and Annie were high school sweethearts who married after they got out of college. They were in their mid-thirties when Annie unexpectedly died as the result of an aneurysm. Bob was beside himself with shock and grief. He was inconsolable. Their years together were happy. Both had good paying jobs and they lived a great life, doing a lot of traveling to many exotic places. They went out to dinner often, drove nice cars, had lots of friends, and enjoyed themselves tremendously.

Annie was only gone for about two months when Bob met Marcy. A few months passed, and things between them developed slowly but steadily. It was a quiet and very comfortable relationship.

On Annie's birthday, Bob posted their wedding photo on Facebook with a message: "Happy Birthday in Heaven, my sweet angel. I love you and will miss you forever."

Many people responded. "Thinking of you, Bob." "Sorry for your loss." "Happy Birthday, Annie. RIP." There were many other similar reactions, along with teary-faced emoticons and emotionally charged memes. There was such an overwhelming outpouring of sympathy and consolation that one would think that Annie had just passed away yesterday and that Bob was all alone in the world instead of happily involved in a relationship with someone else. He loved all the sympathetic attention he was getting.

Marcy was deeply hurt and downright humiliated by all the brouhaha about Annie, but she said nothing to Bob. Instead, she contacted me and dissolved into tears as she told me what happened.

"Don't you see what's happening here?" I asked her. "He's getting all the sympathy, support, and attention of widowhood, plus the comfort, companionship, and other advantages of being in a relationship," I said. "Everybody seems to overlook the fact that he's involved with someone else. It's like you don't even exist! He's getting the best of both worlds. Bob is wearing his widower's halo, playing the grief card, AND getting his needs met with you. He's double-dipping and he'll continue to do so as long as he gets away with it."

That wasn't all. Whenever Marcy went with Bob to spend time with his family and friends, all they talked about was Annie. "They had a once-in-a-lifetime kind of love," one person said. "He'll never love anyone the way he loved Annie," somebody else told Marcy. "Their marriage was like a fairy-tale," another person said. On and on it went that way until Marcy wanted to scream. One night, his friends started talking about Bob and Annie's perfect marriage yet AGAIN and what a terrible loss it was for him when she died.

Marcy finally snapped and said to the group, "It's a good thing Bob and I found each other to fill the void in my life because I still love my ex and I'm on the rebound."

Everybody's mouths dropped open. One of the wives said, "Do you really think it's right to use Bob that way when he's still grieving for Annie?"

Marcy lost it. "Excuse me? Isn't Bob using ME 'that way' while he's still grieving for Annie?"

"But that's different," one of the wives argued. "Bob didn't WANT his marriage to end."

Marcy gave it right back. "I didn't want MY relationship to end, either! Do you think MY loss was any less painful just because it wasn't caused by death?"

Isn't it an outrage the way others put a widower on a pedestal? They expect the new woman in his life to listen with a pleasant, indulgent smile on her face while everyone goes on and on about the late wife. Let's be honest. When a person dies, nobody will badmouth them, even if they were a terrible person. They are far more likely to extol the virtues of the deceased, saying how wonderful and perfect they were. It's almost as if the deceased person is qualified for sainthood. Our society has a weird habit of pretending that people were perfect after they die and glossing over who they really were.

Please, don't get me wrong. It's not right to speak ill of the dead. I have absolutely nothing against people focusing on the good qualities of a person who is no longer with us. The problems begin when such comments are repeated over and over to the woman who falls in love with the surviving spouse of the woman who died. It makes her feel like his Plan B, his second choice, a backup, the default partner, a consolation prize, and the first runner-up who only received the crown because his REAL wife, his FIRST choice, his TRUE love didn't live long enough to finish out her term as his Number One queen. This is a cruel thing to do to the unfortunate woman who came into the widower's life after the late wife died. She feels like a mistress involved with a married man who never intends to leave his wife.

Marcy stopped seeing Bob. She couldn't take the constant humiliation when he openly continued to proclaim his ongoing, never-ending love for Annie on Facebook and in real time. She felt like a cheap imitation who was filling the empty space that Annie left in Bob's life. Sadly, she couldn't fill the empty spot in his heart, and it was too painful for her to try to win this losing battle.

10. WIDOWHOOD VS. DIVORCE

Pain is pain, no matter what causes it. Unfortunately, when someone suffers the loss of a relationship from the death of a spouse, there is no end to the outpouring of patience, sympathy, and support for the surviving partner. People perceive it as normal to spend years grieving for the lost love. The same is not true when a marriage or relationship ends by a breakup or a divorce.

"You're better off without him." "He was a creep." "You'll find somebody better." "Don't waste any more time crying over him." "Snap out of it. It's over." "He wasn't good enough for you." On and on it goes when a woman is grieving over the end of a marriage or relationship. People fail to realize that they're only hurting you further when they minimize your loss and badmouth the person you loved, even if he WAS a jerk. A breakup can be just as traumatic because it's the death of a relationship and a lifestyle. It's the loss of a dream. Nobody gets married or makes a commitment to another person with the idea that it's going to end, any more than a person marries with the thought that their spouse is going to die prematurely. But a divorcee does NOT get the same level of support, understanding, and compassion as the person whose marriage ended in death. Even if the marriage was a terrible one, the fact that the spouse died changes everything. It's a shame that there's such a double standard. The world needs to wake up and respect the fact that heartache comes from many different directions and in a variety of forms. It hurts to lose someone you love, no matter how the loss occurs. Widowers don't own a corner of the market on misery and heartache.

When a man becomes widowed, any bad qualities or behaviors of his deceased spouse are immediately forgotten. She is remembered as saint-like and portrayed as the epitome of perfection, even if she was a horrible person. People are only too happy to share wonderful thoughts and memories of the late wife with her grieving husband. He gets to hear, over and over again, many great things about the wife he lost. Gone are any reminders of her faults, bad habits, and the arguments they had. That all becomes immaterial while the reality of the marriage gets lost in the shuffle. The widower gets to enjoy memories of happy times, and he feels a sense of loss over the fact that his wife is gone. He has the luxury of thinking about her with a sense of longing and nostalgia. This is not the case with a person who is divorced.

When a person is divorced, she isn't as fortunate. HER memories revolve around all the misery and arguments in the marriage. It's not uncommon for people to come up to her and say, "Listen, I didn't want to say anything before, but now that you're divorced, I need to tell you that your husband lied to you, cheated on you, and borrowed money from me behind your back." It's like the divorce decree is a license for others to come out of the woodwork and tell you all kinds of horrible things that you never knew about when you were married to your former husband. Not only are these memories unpleasant, but you're also made to feel like a fool. The marriage leaves you with a bad taste in your mouth. YOU get to think about your ex-husband with feelings of anger and humiliation. YOU get little sympathy or support; instead, you're told how "lucky" you are to have gotten rid of the S.O.B. At this point, you're not about to break down and tell anybody how much you miss him. You'd look like an idiot for crying over the creep. The response you would hear is that you need to "get over it" and "forget about him."

As a result, you suffer in silence. You don't FEEL "lucky" that your ex-husband is gone from your life, but rather, you feel disappointed and disillusioned that things unfolded the way they did. Although you may have wanted the divorce, that wasn't the case when you first got married. You had high hopes and big dreams for that "happily ever after." People often forget about that. A widower, on the other hand, is put on a pedestal and handled with kid gloves because HIS marriage ended "properly," even if the marriage was a sham. I've known of many people whose marriages were hanging by a thread and on the brink of divorce when a spouse died, yet that particular detail becomes conveniently lost in the shuffle.

The loss of a marriage is difficult, no matter HOW it occurs. It's the death of one's hopes and dreams. It leaves a person with a feeling of being cheated out of a future that they were looking forward to. Whether one is widowed or divorced, there's still the burden of starting over, leaving a comfort zone, and having to walk down an unfamiliar path. In my own life, I have experienced both. I have been divorced. I have also been widowed. I must say that being widowed was easier because nobody faulted or judged me for crying and wallowing in the pain of my loss. After I went through a divorce, however, the response I received was very different. People would come up to me and say things like, "It's about time you got rid of him! I can't believe you stayed with him as long as you did. It must feel good to finally have him out of your life. You'll meet somebody better." Nobody told me how sorry they were that things didn't work out. I ended up feeling like an idiot for marrying that person to begin with.

In my humble opinion, getting married is a toss of the dice, the luck of the draw. It's impossible to predict which couples will make it and which ones won't. I have known of several couples who seemed to have it all together and many were shocked when they divorced. Conversely, I've known other couples whose marriages didn't appear to have a snowball's chance in hell of surviving and yet they did. The failure of the marriage should not reflect poorly on the couple who didn't make it, and those whose marriages survived shouldn't be put on a pedestal. Perhaps they were codependent or were afraid of being alone. Maybe they stayed together out of economic necessity or to keep up appearances. These people weren't particularly gifted or special. They just made a decision to stick it out. Perhaps they really loved each other. Lasting marriages have survived infidelity, financial hardships, physical and emotional abuse, and a host of other adversities. Some people have higher tolerance levels than others. Whatever the reasons, the success or failure of a marriage is not a reflection of the people involved.

The head and the heart do not often agree, and the truth is that most people ignore their heads and marry with their hearts. Even if two people are both wonderful, they may end up being totally incompatible. Some people stay together out of fear of being alone or starting over. Then, when the spouse dies, they are held in higher esteem than a divorcee because the marriage stayed intact. There's no guarantee how a marriage will play out. I've known many great couples who did nothing wrong, yet they just couldn't live with each other.

The widower's status earns him respect; a divorcee's status earns her nothing. When somebody gets divorced, their marriages are regarded as failures. The divorcee is criticized for sticking it out for as long as she did until the divorce. When somebody becomes widowed, his or her marriage is considered a "success" because it lasted "'til death do us part." The widower is revered for remaining in the marriage throughout the circumstances that caused the death of his spouse. This is a cruel and unfair double standard. The bottom line is that anyone who survives the end of a marriage deserves equal understanding and support. This should not just be an advantage reserved for those whose marriages end in death. The widower should not be superior to the divorcee.

11. UNRESOLVED GRIEF

As I stated many times, a widower should not be getting involved in another relationship unless and until he has recovered from the death of his late wife. This places an unfair burden on the woman he gets involved with. She is expected to be "understanding, compassionate and patient" while he works through his grief. This was not HER loss, HER grief, or HER set of issues to deal with. She unknowingly walked into a hornet's nest without realizing what she was getting herself into. Like every other human being, the girlfriend, fiancée, or wife of a widower has had her OWN troubles, hardships, and difficulties in life. The last thing she wants to do is to take on someone else's baggage from a previous marriage.

It's not just the unresolved grief that comes with a relationship with a widower. It's also his children who resent you, regular trips to the cemetery, memorial events in the late wife's name, and the potential rocky relationships with her relatives. The new person in the widower's life is put in the position of having to live with the constant presence of another woman, and when she objects, she is regarded as selfish and heartless. She lacks understanding and compassion. She is perceived to be petty, jealous, insecure, and threatened by a dead person.

Newsflash: Women who are in a relationship with a widower are NOT cold-blooded or possessive. All they want is to love and be loved without any residual debris left behind by another woman. They did NOT sign up to be the widower's crying towel or grief counselor. They don't want to be the rebound woman or a shock absorber for his pain. They don't need the aggravation of dealing with all the hostility, rejection, and emotional abuse by his offspring. Would a widower be comforting and supportive while the woman in his life is whining, moaning, and lamenting about the loss of the previous man in HER life? I think not.

Many women don't realize the extent of the widower's ongoing attachment to his late wife until after they have become emotionally invested in the relationship. This puts her in the position of making a difficult decision to either stick it out and hope that the widower gets his act together or ending the relationship and taking the pain and disappointment that comes with it. It comes down to her being forced to choose the lesser of two evils. This is such an unfair predicament for an innocent, unsuspecting woman who was only looking for a normal, meaningful relationship. Instead, she gets dragged into a three-way love triangle that she never signed up for.

Another burden placed on the woman in love with a widower is the feeling of having to compete with a person who is remembered as being 'perfect'. Many widowers have been with their late wives for a very long time; as a result, they are accustomed to thinking of her habits and personality as ideal. ANY woman looks good when she's all a man has ever known. The point is that just because the late wife seemed to be perfect to her surviving spouse, doesn't mean that she was all that great. The widower simply doesn't know anything better and therefore believes that his late wife was the ideal woman, which inadvertently makes his current love interest feel like she's inferior, second-rate, and a second choice.

As I shared earlier, my late husband passed away from a sudden, unexpected and tragic death. It happened only days after our fifth wedding anniversary. Even though I'm a widow myself, I once had somebody tell me that I cannot understand what it's like to lose a spouse after spending decades with him. In other words, I have never been with anyone long enough to understand how much harder it is to recover from a longer lasting bond. That remark was a slap in the face and an insult to the loss of my late husband. I was with my late husband for nearly nine years and married to him for five of those years. We also dated each other back in the 1970s. When I was in my teens, his sister was one of my best friends. I have known my late husband and his family for over thirty-five years, yet my pain was minimized because I was only married to him for five years instead of twenty-five years or more. I don't see it that way. I have been married and divorced, plus I have had other serious, long-term relationships during the course of my life that ended for various reasons. This is not an indication that I am unable to empathize with loss — quite the contrary.

The truth is that I have experienced LOTS of loss, unlike a widower who was married to only one woman for many years. This is the FIRST time he ever experienced the end of a relationship and that's why it seems far more traumatic for him, whereas I have endured the end of MANY relationships over the course of my life. Therefore, I can understand loss and pain far BETTER than a widower who is dealing with the end of a marriage for the first time. Over the years, I have learned how to cope, how to survive, and how to let go of the grief, get my head out of the past, and move on. To suggest that I'm not used to being with one person long enough to build any real bond or that I can't understand what it's like to be widowed after years and years of marriage to the same person is an insult. It trivializes the impact of MY losses and it implies that they were meaningless and less significant by comparison.

12. EUPHORIC RECALL

"Euphoric recall" is a psychological term for the tendency of people to remember past experiences in a positive light, while overlooking negative experiences associated with that situation.

Society just LOVES to romanticize lingering grief. I'm sure many of you have read or heard about how Joe DiMaggio arranged to have roses sent to Marilyn Monroe's grave every week for twenty years after her death, and the public just ate that up! It was such an endearing love story. It was sweet the way Joe DiMaggio pined away for Marilyn Monroe for so long. Sappy, isn't it? It was a true Hollywood love story. In reality, their relationship was a sick, twisted, codependent, tumultuous, adulterous affair, complete with physical and emotional abuse, infidelity, and substance abuse. Marilyn Monroe was well-known for her multiple marriages and illicit affairs. Joe DiMaggio was a jealous, controlling, hotheaded egomaniac. If the average John or Jane Doe engaged in this type of behavior, they would have been regarded as lowlife trash, a slut, man-whore, alcoholic, junkie, etc., but because it was Joe DiMaggio and Marilyn Monroe, their weaknesses, vices, and dysfunctional lifestyles were glamorized and regarded with reverence and a sense of awe. She was America's sweetheart, a movie star, and a sex goddess. He was a superstar sports hero who played his entire career for the New York Yankees. The memories of the drinking, drugging, cheating, physical and emotional abuse, and other bad habits fell by the wayside in deference to their long, ongoing, and charming fixation with each other. Although there were many periods in their lives when they fought like cats and dogs, none of that mattered after Marilyn Monroe died. While the rest of us don't get away with such behavior to that degree, it does happen far more than you think.

Let me tell you a story about a couple and the challenges presented to the next woman who came along after the man's "perfect" wife passed away.

Steve and Elena had a marriage that was considered to be a match made in Heaven. Elena was gorgeous with a body that was the envy of most women, and she had perfect features on her beautiful face. Besides her breathtaking looks, Elena was gregarious and charismatic. Men drooled at the sight of her. Women wanted to BE her. Everyone adored her. She was tastefully flashy — all glitz and glitter and the life of every party. Steve idolized her and was proud to call her his wife.

As the owner of a successful business, Steve was quite affluent. He had more than enough money so that Elena didn't have to go out to work, which was fine by her. She liked her freedom. By the time they had been married for five years, they owned an enormous home and had two adorable little girls. Elena was ever the social butterfly. Marriage and motherhood hadn't slowed her down one bit. Domesticity just didn't agree with her. She enjoyed being around people and she loved to party.

Steve was also aware that Elena was an outrageous flirt, but he always looked the other way, chalking it up to harmless fun. Secretly, it amused him. Deep down, he felt a sense of superiority because Elena was HIS wife. She was a woman who most men would sell their souls to have and HE was the one she chose to marry. As time went on, Elena was home less and less often. She was all about having fun. She lived in the fast lane and enjoyed a life of glamour and excitement. The qualities in Elena that used to excite and fascinate Steve now irritated him. It didn't take long before their marriage started to crumble.

Elena was always coming or going. The children, who were two and four years old by this time, received the bare minimum of her attention and only what was absolutely necessary. Elena hired a woman to take care of the laundry, do the housecleaning, and babysit when she wanted to go out. Being a wife and mother was not "her thing" she told Steve. She wasn't a warm and fuzzy person. It was not uncommon for her to get all dressed up and go out for a few drinks during "happy hour," not coming home until the wee hours of the morning. She was always partying. Her drinking got worse and worse. Steve and Elena fought constantly. Her way of dealing with marital tension was to leave the house whenever an argument broke out and not return home for hours.

It was also not uncommon for Elena to go off on a "girls' getaway," running off to Las Vegas or some exotic island vacation, leaving Steve alone for extended periods of time to care for the children.

One day, after Elena had returned from yet another one of her many excursions, Steve found photos in her phone of her with another man, taken only days earlier on a white sand beach standing by a body of beautiful turquoise water. They were wearing swimsuits and in some of the photos, Elena was topless. The man with Elena had his arms around her, and it was obvious they were lovers. He turned out to be Elena's regular "traveling companion." Elena obviously wasn't going away with "the girls." That wasn't all. There were many whispered phone calls and Elena became increasingly more secretive. Steve wasn't stupid. He knew that Elena was having an affair and it was probably not the first time she had cheated on him. It angered and humiliated him. He was sick and tired of this empty, loveless farce of a marriage. He worked all day, only to come home to an empty house with a meal for him and the girls that had been prepared by the hired woman. The children were clingy and starved for love and attention. During the day, Elena's time was spent shopping, getting massages, having her hair and nails done, and doing God knows what else.

Steve's many efforts to work things out with Elena were all to no avail. He finally had enough and told Elena that they needed to sit down and talk about some changes that needed to be made if they were going to save their marriage. Elena became instantly defensive and accused Steve of trying to keep her on a tight leash. It escalated into another argument with Elena storming off, saying that Steve was putting too much pressure on her and that she was going out for a few drinks to unwind. As she slammed the door on her way out, Steve was determined to sit Elena down to tell her that if she didn't work harder on their marriage, he was going to end it — but that scenario wasn't meant to be. That night, Elena was intoxicated and on her way home from her favorite cocktail lounge, when she hit a concrete road barrier at a high rate of speed, causing her car to flip over a couple of times before landing upside down on the highway. No other cars were involved and nobody was hurt except Elena…she was killed instantly.

Steve always feared that something like this might happen. Elena's drinking had started to get progressively worse. It was inevitable that it would come to a head one of these days. In spite of their marital problems, Steve was crushed because he still loved Elena and was just as attracted to her as ever. She was like an elusive butterfly that he couldn't hold on to. Still, he nursed the belief that they were just going through a rough patch and that things would get better in time. He was willing to forgive her for everything, including the cheating, if only she would try to make their marriage work. Another part of Steve was resigned when he dared to be honest enough with himself to admit that the marriage was too far gone to salvage.

In any event, Elena was just as vivacious in death as in life. There was barely enough room for the large assortment of flowers in the funeral home; there was a long procession of mourners extending halfway down the street, waiting to come inside to pay their last respects. One person after another offered their condolences to Steve, telling him how lucky he was to have been married to such a special person, that she was beautiful, charismatic and would be deeply missed. On and on it went, as people shared endless anecdotes of all their wonderful memories of Elena. To hear them talk, one would think that she was qualified for sainthood.

As with any death, everyone goes back to their own lives after the funeral. Once all the hoopla had settled down, Steve found himself thinking about Elena all the time when he was alone at night, after the girls were asleep. He often looked through the photos taken during various periods of his life with Elena, fondly reminiscing about how mesmerized he was the first time he ever laid eyes on her and the way she lit up a room with her beauty and sparking personality. He smiled to himself, as he thought back to the way he chased her shamelessly just to get a date with her. At the time, he knew he was making a fool out of himself, but he didn't care. He intended to have her at any cost. He was walking on air when she accepted his marriage proposal. The reality and finality of her death hit him like a ton of bricks. Steve's grief gave way to gut-wrenching sobs. His beautiful, precious Elena was gone forever.

A handsome, successful, young widower is always an appealing prospect to a woman who has no idea what she's getting herself into. Steve was a great catch, obviously a committed family man — financially stable, excellent marriage material, and since he was widowed, there would be no ex-wife to deal with. This was what Courtney was thinking when Steve asked her out. They both worked in the same office building, but at that time, Courtney had no idea that he was the owner of the company where he worked every day. Steve was very laid back, down to Earth, and to look at him, you would think he was just like any other regular working guy. He and Courtney knew each other casually and would often say "good morning" and stop to chat for a few minutes when they ran into each other from time to time. Courtney was attractive in a clean, quiet way. She dressed nicely, but not with the snappy, high-fashion kind of clothing Elena was known to wear. Steve invited Courtney out for a drink one evening after work only a few months after Elena's death. Courtney listened sympathetically as Steve spilled his guts, telling her about some of their marital frustrations that nobody else knew about. From all outward appearances, Steve and Elena had the perfect marriage; most people would have been shocked had they known what was really going on. Courtney was a fantastic listener and it was a relief for Steve to be able to open up and get everything off his chest until he finally ended by telling Courtney about the chain of events that led to Elena's untimely death.

Steve and Courtney's relationship took off quickly after that moment. She adored his little girls and they loved her, as well. They were too young to remember much about Elena, especially since she paid little attention to them. Less than a year later, Courtney gave up her apartment and moved into Steve's house. Unlike Elena, Courtney was very family oriented. She cleaned, cooked, and did the laundry. The house became a home — warm, inviting, comfortable, and secure. The children blossomed under Courtney's loving care. She was the mother they never had. Sadly, the fairy tale didn't last. Elena's presence was still all over the house. Her large assortment of clothing, shoes, and lingerie filled the closets and drawers. The smell of her heavy, expensive perfume permeated the bedroom. Her cosmetics and exclusive jewelry sat untouched right where Elena left them. Courtney saw Elena's intimidating beauty everywhere she looked. Elena had done some modeling in earlier years and had been extremely photogenic. She loved having her picture taken, which Courtney saw on the walls of every room in the house, where Elena was hamming it up, flashing her extensive wardrobe as she playfully switched from one pose to another for the camera and wearing everything from a bikini to formal attire.

That wasn't all. Whenever Courtney and Steve got together with his family and friends, she had to listen to an endless barrage of stories about Elena. "You would have liked her...she was so gorgeous and exciting. It's a shame you never had a chance to meet her. Everybody admired her." Elena's presence haunted Courtney constantly. There's more. Both of Steve's young daughters were the spitting image of their mother, a fact that people made it a point to mention all the time. "Those little girls are going to be pretty like their mother. Nobody was more beautiful than Elena."

Courtney was becoming increasingly more uncomfortable with these unintentional blows, so she decided to talk to Steve. "Don't you think it's time to get rid of Elena's things? She's in my face constantly. I would feel more comfortable if her photos were removed and packed away. This house doesn't feel like mine. It's almost as if I'm living in another woman's home and sleeping with another woman's husband," she told him.

Steve didn't see it that way. "Courtney, the girls are so young. This is all they have left of their mother. If I remove Elena's photos and her belongings, it's as if I'm wiping out all traces of the girls' mother. I want to keep Elena's memory alive, for THEIR sake, so that they don't forget her."

If that wasn't bad enough, it was obvious that Steve still loved and missed Elena. He continued to wear his wedding ring. He broke down into tears on her birthday, the date of her death, their wedding anniversary, and other significant dates. Courtney had long ago stopped offering Steve her sympathetic support when he started crying the blues about Elena. She was sick and tired of hearing about her. Courtney felt that it was unfair that Steve didn't get Elena out of his system, before deciding to get involved with her. She began to feel like a bandage for his wounded heart and a proxy for the spot that Elena vacated. Courtney felt like she was second choice, the default lover who was only there because Elena couldn't be. She simply stepped into Elena's life and picked right up where Steve and Elena left off, losing herself in the process. Courtney cleaned THEIR house, cooked meals in THEIR kitchen, did THEIR laundry, slept in THEIR bed, cared for THEIR children, and all the while, Steve continued wearing his wedding band and grieving for Elena. This is referred to as a "three-hearts relationship"...the widower, his late wife, and his current love interest. Courtney had Elena's life but Elena had Steve's heart and it seemed that she always would.

The most significant point of this situation was that Steve seemed to have forgotten all about Elena's drinking, her emotional indifference, her unavailability, her apathy toward him and the girls, her reckless, irresponsible partying, excessive spending, selfishness, and last but not least, her infidelity. Elena was kept on a pedestal and remembered as the epitome of perfection — the ideal wife and mother...sexy, beautiful, charismatic, and exciting, instead of the lying, cheating, drinking, uncaring mother and unfaithful wife that she was. This is a classic case of "euphoric recall."

Courtney ended up moving out of Steve's house and ending her relationship with him, leaving his little girls heartbroken. Courtney could not have loved these children more than if they were her own; however, if she stayed and accepted Steve's mediocre devotion to her, she would have lost her self-respect in the process.

13. GASLIGHTING

Many of you have heard of "gaslighting." It's a form of manipulation used to sow seeds of doubt, causing you to question your own beliefs, perception, and even your sanity. It's a tactic where the abuser uses persistent denial, misdirection, contradiction, and even outright lying. The intention is to destabilize you, minimize and trivialize your feelings, cause you to second-guess yourself, and make you wonder if you're losing your mind.

This is a form of emotional abuse that is not unique to a widower; however, when you are subject to this type of treatment on top of other late wife-related issues, it's enough to drive you out of your mind.

Tony and Kathy's relationship is a good example of gaslighting. Tony was a widower with three children. He met Kathy a few months after his wife Laura died from cancer. Tony was still very much attached to his late wife, and his relationship with Kathy always took a backseat to anything related to Laura. This didn't become obvious to Kathy until she and Tony had been in a relationship for about six months. Either she didn't notice or Tony kept that fact hidden until he was sure that Kathy was fully committed to him. In any event, it was very upsetting to her when she finally realized the extent of Tony's dedication to Laura. Everything in Tony's life revolved around Laura and although Kathy bit her tongue, she finally spoke up after it all came to a head.

It happened on Laura's birthday. The children wanted to throw their late mother a party at the house. Tony not only encouraged it, but he also helped arrange it, and he went all out. His family was invited, as were his former in-laws. Kathy, too, was welcome and she decided to attend, not knowing just how awkward it was going to be. The house was full of birthday decorations and balloons, all in different shades of purple — Laura's favorite color. Tony had an assortment of Laura's favorite foods and snacks. Her favorite songs were playing in the background. There was even an empty chair at the head of the table with a large photo of Laura sitting on it. It was almost as if Laura herself was there at the party. As soon as everybody finished eating, they sat around the table and took turns sharing their favorite memories of Laura. On and on it went, while Kathy sat and had to listen to one person after another talk about what a great wife, mother, sister, daughter, and aunt Laura had been, how special she was, her extraordinary cooking and baking abilities, her impeccable housekeeping skills, her successful and well-paying job, her envious sense of style, her upbeat attitude, high energy level, popularity, well-loved personality, etc. Worst of all, there were several comments about Laura being "one of a kind," "second to none," and "irreplaceable." Finally, after everyone was finished, they gathered around the cake, sang "Happy Birthday" to Laura and after the three children blew out the candles, everybody went outside to release the large assortment of balloons into the air as they wished Laura a "Happy Birthday up in Heaven."

Kathy felt humiliated. She felt as small, inferior, and insignificant as a human being could possibly be. As soon as she could do so inconspicuously, Kathy left. After she got into her car and drove away, she dissolved into tears, crying with deep, gasping sobs. At home she took a shower, put on a nightgown, went to bed, and cried all night long. All she could think about was how deeply she cared about Tony and the fact that he still loved Laura, probably always would and, worst of all, would never love HER with that same degree of intensity.

After a restless night, Kathy got up and went to work. Later that morning, Tony called her. "Wasn't that a great party, hon? Laura would have loved it. I'm so glad you were able to join us!" The way he said that made her feel like just another invited guest instead of the woman he was in a relationship with. "Anyway," he went on, "why don't you come to my house after work? We can have a bite to eat and spend some time together."

Kathy agreed, but she planned to have a talk with him about the way he continued living in the past. It was time for him to let go of Laura, to move on and focus on his relationship with HER.

When Kathy got to Tony's house, he was a bit distracted and the house was a mess. "Sorry I don't have anything ready for us to eat," he apologized. "I didn't expect the party to end as late as it did and I was too tired afterwards to clean up. The kids were no help, either. Maybe you can help me with this mess and then I'll warm up some of the party leftovers in the microwave and we can eat."

Inwardly, Kathy was fuming. Once again, she was getting someone's "leftovers" and she was sick to death of it. She seethed silently as she tackled a sink full of dirty dishes, threw away paper party plates with bits of dried cake and icing stuck on them, picked up pieces of party favors, bits of broken balloons and threw them all in the trash. She ran the dishwasher, then swept and vacuumed up the crumbs and food that had dropped all over the place. She wrapped up the soiled tablecloth, shook it outside, and threw it in with the dirty laundry and ran the washing machine. Finally, she sat down with Tony, who barely lifted a finger, letting HER do most of the dirty work. Kathy had worked all day and now this. She was exhausted, furious, hungry, and ready to explode.

"Kath, if you don't mind, why don't you throw some food in the microwave, will you? Let's relax a while. It's been a long day."

Kathy snapped and unleashed a tirade of her long held, pent-up frustrations. She went on about how she was sick and tired of being treated like a maid and a whore. She helped him with his kids, cleaned his house, provided him with plenty of sex, and companionship, yet Laura was the love of his life and she would always have his heart. "AND THAT RIDICULOUS PARTY — DEAD PEOPLE DON'T HAVE ANY MORE BIRTHDAYS!" she screamed.

Tony looked at her in shocked disbelief and then ripped into her about her selfishness. "First of all," he yelled, that birthday party wasn't so much for Laura, but for my three kids who needed to hang onto the memory of their mother. It was THEIR idea to have this party; I only went along with it to make them happy! How can you begrudge them that? Furthermore, you have to remember that her family is still grieving and it brought them some comfort to know that she wasn't being forgotten. Finally, MY family couldn't have loved her more if she was blood-related and they enjoyed bringing her spirit back to life, if only for a little while. How can you be so damn shallow and self-centered? It was only for a few hours out of one friggin' day of our lives! Are you really so petty that you can't put your own selfishness aside for a little while for the sake of a heartbroken family? You know something, Kathy? You're making this all about YOU! Don't you think you're overreacting? You're way too sensitive. You're blowing this whole thing out of proportion. It was only a birthday party, for God's sake!"

Kathy's head started spinning. Was she REALLY making a mountain out of a mole hill? She didn't HAVE to clean up the party mess, she reminded herself. She could have just told Tony that she was tired and wanted to stay home instead of going over and wearing herself out whipping his house back into shape. Maybe she DID create her own problems and then blame him. "Look, Tony, I'm sorry I blew up at you.

Maybe I'm overly tired. I just need to go home and get a good night's sleep. I'm sure I'll feel better tomorrow."

As she drove home, she started second-guessing herself. She WAS exhausted; she was SO upset about the party yesterday that she barely got any sleep that night. Could Tony be right about her overreacting? She stopped at a fast-food drive-thru, grabbed some take-out, and went home, where she continued to wonder whether Tony's anger toward her was justified or if her dissatisfaction and resentment were legitimate. She couldn't think straight at this point.

I told her that she wasn't crazy and that she wasn't overreacting. What was happening, I explained, was that Tony was gaslighting her. She went out of her way for him and his kids, often putting their feelings and needs ahead of her own. In return, Tony continually treated her with disrespect, reserving all his love and loyalty for Laura. Kathy made her relationship with Tony a priority while he treated her as if she were a secondary option, and then when she confronted him about it, he dismissed her complaints, suggesting that they were all in her head, adding insult to injury. He was causing her to doubt herself to the point where she started to ignore her gut feelings and mistrust her instincts. SHE was the injured party, yet TONY was the one acting like the victim.

"You don't deserve this, but a good bit of it is your fault," I gently told her. Tony was keeping their relationship on the back burner, then turning it around to make Kathy feel like she was "overly emotional," "too sensitive," or "twisting things around," which is the epitome of gaslighting. This is not a tactic unique to a widower, but rather the actions of a narcissist. Being with a widower is difficult enough, but being with a torch bearing widower who is gaslighting you is a double whammy. There's no working through this one. Better to get away from such a man — fast!

Kathy gave far too much to Tony, while he offered her far too little in return. When she made an attempt to talk to him about it, he quashed her voice and belittled her concerns, causing her to question and doubt herself. Whether Kathy's feelings were credible or not is beside the point. The fact is that Tony didn't seem to care or take them seriously. He just blew her off like she was being a nuisance.

After I spoke with Kathy, she felt validated and relieved that she wasn't losing her mind. Her confidence and self-respect returned and she ended up breaking up with Tony. "You have a right to hang on to Laura forever, if that's what you want," she told him, "but the deal is that I am ALSO entitled to do what makes ME happy. I'm always feeling like a poor second to Laura, like I'm only an afterthought. Whether or not you think it's all in my head is beside the point. The fact is that my needs aren't being met or even taken into consideration. You will be better off finding a woman who doesn't mind living in Laura's shadow, and I will be better off with a man who lives in the present, so I have decided to tell you goodbye."

For a minute, Tony was speechless. When he regained his composure, he told her that she was f--ked up.

"If that's what you believe, then we really ARE better off ending this relationship," she calmly and firmly told him. "Stop gaslighting me, Tony. I'm onto you. Good luck. I hope your memories keep you warm at night. Please give your kids my best." And with that, she walked away from Tony with her head held high.

Kathy thanked me for saving her sanity.

"I only gave you my opinion and a few suggestions," I replied. "YOU are the one who took the necessary but difficult steps to free yourself from this sick, twisted relationship. You don't give yourself any credit. You need to learn how to recognize and appreciate your incredible courage and strength."

Kathy's experience was a painful one and as a result she was very wary of men who were widowed. Happily, she met a nice guy about a year later, and yes, Jeff was also a widower, but his attitude was that life is for the living and if he was lucky enough to find somebody special, he was going to grab onto her with both hands and keep her close to his heart, knowing that he would be richly blessed if he were to get another chance at love. His actions were as good as his words. There were no lingering grief fests, no posthumous birthday parties, no shrines and no torch-bearing activities. Jeff showed Kathy how much he loved and appreciated her in every way possible. His life and focus were on the present, not the past. He put Kathy on a pedestal and after two years of dating, they got married and have been very happy ever since.

She cringes when she thinks about what her life would have been like if she had stayed with Tony. "You have to accept the pain of letting go of what you have in order to free yourself up for something better. I know that now, and I thank God I learned this valuable lesson before I made a terrible mistake," she told me. "Jeff is the best thing that ever happened to me."

Judging by the happy smile on her face and the sparkle in her eyes, I couldn't agree more.

14. THE PLACEHOLDER

A "placeholder" is the person whom a widower dates, sleeps with, gets involved with, or even marries when he is unable to do so with the love of his life.

No woman wants to feel like she's getting the late wife's seconds. This is especially true when the widower is incapable of letting go of the past. In cases like this, the widower's intention is not to move on and start a new chapter, but rather to pick up right where he left off with his late wife. All he needs is a willing participant. He doesn't come right out and say this, but that's what he's looking for. Perhaps he doesn't even realize it himself. Such a situation doesn't come to light until a meaningful relationship is starting to become established.

Take Ed, for example. He and Helen, his late wife, were married for forty-three years when she died of a heart attack. Her sudden death left Ed in a complete state of shock and emotional disarray. His life had been so deeply enmeshed with Helen's that he couldn't even think straight. They had the kind of marriage where they did everything together; you rarely saw one of them without the other. What made it worse was that they were never able to have any children, so they were even more interdependent than most other couples. While this degree of closeness is enviable and not very common these days, it's never a good idea to put all your eggs in one basket, so to speak. It's always a wise idea to maintain one's own interests, and activities; otherwise, there will be little to nothing to fall back on should the marriage come to an end.

Such was the case with Ed. He and Helen had married right out of high school and were almost like Siamese twins, and when she died Ed was dangerously despondent. His was not the usual, normal grief of losing a spouse — he was literally unable to function. Those who were closest to Ed worried about what would become of him. Many people predicted that he would not survive much longer without her. It wasn't just Helen who died. Ed's life died with her.

You can only imagine everyone's utter shock and disbelief when Ed started seeing a woman only two months later. Betsy was actually one of Helen's former classmates who got together with Helen from time to time. They had remained friendly since high school and stayed in touch, so when Betsy heard about Helen's passing, she reached out to Ed to extend her condolences and to ask how he was holding up. Ed broke down and started sobbing. Once the floodgates opened, he couldn't stop crying. Betsy's heart went out to him. She, too, was a widow, but unlike Ed's marriage to Helen, hers was not a happy one. Neil was an alcoholic who had made her life a living hell. She always feared that he would either kill himself or someone else because of his habit of driving while he was severely intoxicated.

The day came when Betsy finally got the call she had been dreading. It had been raining very heavily all night and visibility was poor. Neil had spent several hours in a bar and was so drunk when he left that he could barely stand up, much less drive. He lost control of his car, drove it right through a park and smashed into a tree. He was badly injured and lingered in a coma for about a week before he slipped away. Betsy's only consolation was that he didn't injure or kill an innocent person along with himself. At first, their marriage was a happy one until Neil's drinking got out of control; still, she never gave up hope that he would sober up. But that never happened. In spite of the pain of losing him, his death was somewhat of a relief. She decided to make a fresh new start. She sold their house and moved into a nice apartment in a nearby neighborhood. She needed to get away from all the bad memories and get on with her life. This had happened several years earlier; by this time, Betsy's life was a peaceful and happy one, although not terribly exciting.

When Betsy realized how broken up Ed was over Helen's death, her heart went out to him, as she was no stranger to sorrow herself. She invited him over for dinner and he accepted. It was comforting for him to enjoy a home-cooked meal. Betsy was warm and sympathetic, listening to him with understanding and compassion as he poured his heart out about his struggle to survive without Helen. This was how it started. After that dinner, things between them developed rather quickly — TOO quickly, everyone thought. Within three months of seeing each other, at Ed's suggestion, Betsy gave up her apartment and moved into his house. Ed was like a new man — it was like somebody gave him his life back, but like other couples who enjoy the novelty of a new relationship, the pink cloud didn't last.

The earliest sign of trouble was when Betsy made dinner for them in Ed's kitchen for the first time. As they were eating the lasagna she prepared, Ed offered to give Betsy Helen's lasagna recipe, which he described as "off the cuff."

Betsy was hurt. "What's wrong with MY lasagna?" she asked.

"Oh, not a thing. It's just not what I'm used to," he explained.

Betsy bit her tongue. After all, Helen had only been gone for five months. Ed just needed a little more time to adjust, she told herself.

That was only the beginning. Ed objected to everything that Betsy did that was different from Helen, even to the way she replaced the toilet paper. Betsy always placed the toilet paper so that it hung over the top only to notice that Ed changed it so that it was under the bottom. "This was the way Helen always put it on," he told Betsy. He insisted on keeping things exactly the way they were when Helen was alive.

Ed wanted to go places and do things with Betsy that he and Helen used to enjoy. He even offered to introduce her to some of Helen's other friends. "You'll like them," he promised. That wasn't all. Ed had the nerve to push her to watch certain TV shows. "We watch this all the time," he told her. By "we" he was referring to himself and Helen. He always spoke of her in the present tense, often using the term "we" as if they were still a couple.

Ed went so far as to let Betsy know that she was "welcome" to Helen's wardrobe. "She dressed nicely and she was about the same size as you," he told Betsy.

"What's wrong with MY clothes and the way I dress?" she demanded to know.

"Not a thing," he assured her. "It's just a shame to let all those nice clothes, shoes, and handbags sit there going to waste."

Betsy tried another tactic. "If you'd like, I'll help you to pack up Helen's belongings and donate them. There are several charitable organizations that would greatly benefit from these nice things, and they'll be put to good use by people who really need them."

"Give away Helen's things? Oh, I couldn't bear for them to end up with strangers. I'd much rather see YOU have them," Ed said magnanimously. The way Ed said it made it sound like he was giving Betsy a special gift!

It was a bad situation. Ed was slowly and steadily chipping away at Betsy piece by piece. It felt like Ed was trying to turn her into Helen! It was infuriating and frustrating. She had to face the painful realization that in Ed's mind and heart, he was still very much married to Helen. The problem was that Helen was no longer around. Ed desperately needed to fill the vacancy that Helen left behind and unconsciously felt that the best candidate would be someone who knew and liked Helen. He jumped at the first available woman who expressed any concern for him and unwittingly tried to force her into picking right up where Helen left off. Ed rejected anything and everything different from what Helen said or did. It was a tremendous and unfair burden to place on Betsy or ANY woman, for that matter. By his actions, what he was saying in effect was, "I can only love you if you can provide me with an almost identical substitute for what I lost when Helen died."

Betsy was heartbroken, but she wasn't devastated. Experience taught her not to wait around, hoping Ed would change. She wasted a lot of years with Neil, expecting and trusting that he would sober up so that she could have the happiness she envisioned. She wasn't about to make that same mistake again. Ed was a decent guy and, for the most part, was kind and generous to her. His biggest and only flaw was that he didn't see or appreciate Betsy for who she was, but rather her potential to bring Helen back to life, so to speak. Ed rejected her cooking, her manner of dress, her daily habits, and her TV preferences if they differed from Helen's. It was too great a price to pay. She wasn't loved for who she was. She was simply a placeholder for Helen, and she couldn't live like that — not if she wanted to keep her own identity.

She explained all of this to Ed as she packed up her belongings. "I like you, Ed. You're a great guy, but you are clearly not over Helen and you may never be. I can understand why you loved her so much. I'd known her for many years and I liked her. She was a wonderful woman. It's sad that she died. I know how much you miss her. I'm sure you'd give anything to be with her again, but the fact is that she's gone and she's never coming back. Ever. You don't see me as anything more than an extension of Helen. She and I had a lot in common, but we were also different in many ways. It's those differences that you can't bear to face.

"I can't stop being who I am in order to give you back what you lost. I would be doing myself an incredible injustice. You're not finished grieving and there's nothing wrong with that. You never really gave yourself enough time to come to terms with Helen's passing. I get that, I really do. I blame myself. You weren't thinking clearly, so I should have been the one who recognized this and kept a certain distance from you instead of jumping into a relationship with you only two months after Helen died. We can remain friendly and even get together once in a while for coffee or dinner, but I can't be romantically involved with you. I hope I meet somebody special someday who can give me what I want, but even if I don't, I can be happy — as long as my self-respect remains intact. I refuse to lose myself in a relationship again. As the old expression goes, I would rather be hated for who I am than loved for who I'm not. Take care of yourself, Ed. I really and truly wish you only the best, but I can no longer stay with you on your terms. I hope you understand."

Ed listened to Betsy intently and without interruption. Finally, he said,

"I have to admit that much of what you said is true. Even now, I have a very uncomfortable and stressful feeling inside at the knowledge that I'm going to be alone again. It's something that I'm not used to. Helen and I were together for most of our lives and I don't know how to be by myself, but I also get what you're saying. Believe me when I tell you that it was never my intention to hurt you or to have any disregard for your feelings. I guess I'm out of practice here. Helen is really the only woman I've ever known and it never occurred to me to think about what my actions were doing to you. I'm so sorry, Betsy. I truly am. My cruelty wasn't deliberate. You've been incredibility patient with me. Maybe I do need to get my head on straight first before I do anything else. I just don't know how to go about it. I have no idea where to start. I thought that I was healing by getting involved in a new relationship, but I guess I was just hiding behind you and putting a bandage on my wounded heart."

Betsy knew that his words were sincere. *Hurt people hurt people*, she reminded herself.

After Betsy moved out of Ed's house, she stayed with her son and daughter-in-law for a few months until she found another apartment that she liked. Ed still calls her and they even get together from time to time, but their relationship is a platonic one that provides them both with occasional companionship and an escort for social and couple-oriented functions. Ed and Betsy are both nice people, but that doesn't mean that two nice people can make it as a couple. Betsy wanted to be in a relationship where she was loved and appreciated for who she was. Ed wanted to bring Helen back to life. It was a recipe for failure. Fortunately, they were able to resolve the problem peacefully. They developed a warm but casual friendship that worked for both of them.

Some relationships, even with the best intentions, do not work out, and the right thing to do is to face it and handle it the best way possible. There is only pain and disappointment to be had by staying with the wrong person and trying to turn him or her into the right one.

Whether Ed and Betsy will give it another try down the road remains to be seen. Lesson learned: When getting involved with a widower, make sure that he's truly over his late wife and that it is YOU he wants.

15. FACEBOOK TAGS

This is, by far, another one of the most common complaints that I hear from women who become involved with men whose wives have died. Even if your widowed partner doesn't post anything about his late wife on Facebook, it doesn't stop other people from doing so and then "tagging" him in the post. This happens on many different occasions: the late wife's birthday, the date of her death, Mothers' Day, Christmas, and, last but not least, their wedding anniversary. That in itself is hard enough to look at, but then there are the photos of your man and his late wife followed by several expressions of sympathy, as if his grief was still fresh and raw.

No woman wants to read emotional anecdotes about her man and his late wife, or any other woman, for that matter. She doesn't want to see photos of the two of them together. Most importantly, she doesn't want to see expressions of comfort, support, and sympathy. That would be tantamount to suggesting that he's still grieving for his late wife. It also sends a subliminal message that the late wife is irreplaceable and that the current woman in the widower's life will always be a poor substitute and a second choice. Even if the woman isn't friends with any of these people, she will see their comments if they tag her widower in their commiserating Facebook posts.

Another major complaint that I hear repeatedly is about what the widower himself puts on Facebook. This is especially common during the late wife's birthday, the date of their former wedding anniversary, her date of death, or other significant events. Take Jake, for example. On Christmas morning, he posted a message on Facebook to Marion, his late wife: "Merry

Christmas, my darling. The holidays will never be the same without you."

When Ginny, his fiancée saw that, she was devastated and humiliated. He had just told the entire world that he was still thinking of Marion and missing her. In effect, Jake's comments gave the reader the impression that Ginny would never be good enough, that Jake would never be truly satisfied with anyone but Marion. Even worse, Jake never posted anything on Facebook about enjoying Christmas with Ginny. If he wanted to post ANYTHING, it should have been directed to Ginny ("Merry Christmas, my darling. The holidays are extra special because of you.").

When she tried to explain this to Jake, he was genuinely baffled. "But Marion's dead. I'm with YOU now; it's not like I'm ever going to be with Marion again, and it makes people feel good to know that I haven't forgotten about her."

What Ginny heard was that the ONLY reason Jake was with her was because he couldn't have Marion. In so many words, Jake had told her that she would be the default wife — the first-runner up who only received the crown because the REAL queen of his life didn't live long enough to serve her full term.

Ginny couldn't understand why it was Jake's responsibility to pacify the people who wanted him to hang on to Marion. Jake didn't want to "upset" Marion's loved ones by making it appear as if she was forgotten, but it was apparently okay to upset Ginny by nursing their grief. All he was doing was making Ginny feel like she was second best. Jake just didn't get it. The sad truth is that most people don't. The hardest part is that the new woman in a widower's life is often expected to be pleasantly tolerant in the midst of constant reminders of the woman who came before her. She is supposed to sit back and plaster a happy smile on her face, as he lovingly prances down Memory Lane. All she wants is for him to live in the here and now, loving HER. What's wrong with that? Is that really too much to ask? This is what everybody wants and deserves. Just because the man in her life is widowed doesn't mean that she should settle for anything less than what any other self-respecting woman has a right to expect from the man she loves.

These kinds of Facebook activities make the widower's current woman feel small, insignificant, and as inadequate as humanly possible. Furthermore, as I've stated repeatedly, if a widower is still feeling the sorrow and pain of his late wife's death, it's a self-centered move on his part to use another woman to fulfill the needs that his late wife isn't around to satisfy. If he HAS recovered from his loss enough to let go and move on, he needs to let the torch bearers know that he doesn't appreciate their attempts to drag him back down there with them. Perhaps they resent that he isn't mired in misery over his late wife's death and, instead, has a new and happy relationship with someone else. Maybe they aren't ready to see him letting go of the past in order to fully embrace the life he has today. It could also be a painful indication that their loved one is being forgotten and fading further and further into the past. Maybe they are still feeling the void of the late wife's absence. That's fine, but if the widower has made it clear that he's happy again and wants to move on, they need to find someone else to join them in their grief fests. They have absolutely no right to drag anybody else down with them.

Many widowers won't "untag" themselves from these postings for fear they'll hurt those who created these Facebook memorial comments and photos, yet they are hurting their current love interest by NOT removing themselves from these tags. I have a solution that could be a win-win for all concerned. The widower can set up his Facebook account so that he has to approve all posts where he is tagged before they can appear on his Facebook page. If he doesn't provide his approval, it won't stop these things from being on Facebook, but it won't show up on HIS Facebook page. Best of all, the person who tags him won't have the power to clutter his Facebook page with anything that the widower didn't choose to post himself.

The late wife isn't going to see what her widower does or does not do on Facebook. When his sentiment for her is demonstrated to be stronger than his love and respect for the woman he is with now, that is a problem.

In my research, women in love with widowers have all told me the same thing. The man's reactions are always the same: "But she's no threat to you because she's DEAD. Why are you so worked up over someone who can never come back?"

Obviously, they don't understand. The partner of a widower doesn't feel "threatened" by the late wife. She just believes that, given the option, the man she loves would prefer to be with his late wife instead of with her. It's hurtful and humiliating to think that he's only with her by chance and not by choice.

Bottom line: Into each life a little rain must fall. No human being on this Earth will ever go through life without pain and loss. A widower's sorrow is no worse than that of anyone else who loses a loved one. There have been people who have suffered the worst kind of heartache of all: the death of a child. As a rule, people don't try to keep reminding them of the child they lost. In most cases, people support the bereaved, and when they see a grief-stricken person having a good day, they are generally encouraging and careful not to say anything that would remind them of their loss, yet the same doesn't immediately apply to the man who lost his wife. There seems to be some kind of unspoken conspiracy to keep him grieving, tied to the late wife and to mistreat the unfortunate woman who dares to fall in love with him. It's an unfair burden to put on someone, let alone the widower who is over his late wife and has found his way back to happiness.

As one woman put it, "My widower's late wife gets rubbed in our faces whenever people tag him in Facebook posts on any significant days. People want to drag him back down, hoping to keep him in his grief because they are not ready to see him move on."

If someone wants to stay stuck in their sadness, by all means, let them do so, but they need to understand that these are THEIR feelings and that they need to stop tagging and dragging the now-happy widower down with them.

16. THE PAST VS. THE PRESENT

There's a common mindset in the many widowers whose former marriage to the late wife was a happy one: He's reluctant to do better by you than he did for the late wife. Let me explain by sharing the following example.

Cindy asked Lou, her fiancé, to go to Atlantic City with her. She absolutely loved the casino atmosphere…the bright lights, the shows, the food, the ocean, the boardwalk, and the devilish risks and imagined rewards of the table games and slot machines. It was exciting to her. Lou adamantly refused to go, saying that it wasn't "his thing."

Cindy tried to talk him into it. "But how can you be sure that you won't like it? You've never been there. There is so much to see and do. There's something there for everybody. Keep an open mind, Lou. You might actually enjoy yourself. Even if you don't think you'll have fun, why not just do it for me?"

Lou wouldn't budge. "Leave it alone, Cindy, will you? I don't want to go and that's that. I'm not going to change my mind."

Naturally, an argument broke out, with Cindy complaining that Lou was being selfish. "This is what couples do, Lou. They make sacrifices for each other. I'm not asking you to become a degenerate gambler. I just thought we'd go for the weekend, see a show or two, have dinner, take a stroll on the boardwalk, and maybe play some slots or table games. It would do us good to get away and take a break from our routine. Why are you being so stubborn about this?"

Lou said, "Cindy, I'm not that dead set against going to Atlantic City. It's just that Judy must have asked me a million times to go with her when she was alive and I refused. I can remember her literally begging me to go to Atlantic City with her to the point of tears, but I never went with her — not even once. Now if I agree to go with YOU and my kids found out about it, they would be very upset that I went there with you when I wouldn't go with their mother!"

Cindy nearly lost it. "I don't give a rat's ass about that! Whatever you did with Judy should NOT set the tone for what you do with ME! Should I be penalized because of something that happened in the past, before you met me? If you want to go to Atlantic City, then what's stopping you? Are you going to let the past control the present?"

Lou didn't back down. "Just drop it, Cindy. If I went to Atlantic City, it would upset my kids. They remember how many times Judy bugged me to go. I just can't do it!"

"Okay, Lou. Fine. I'm not about to beg and plead with you the way Judy did. Have it your way." Cindy dropped it, but she was seething inside. Once again, Judy's memory was contaminating her relationship with Lou. Because of something that happened between Lou and Judy during their marriage, she was going to be disadvantaged and it wouldn't be the first time. Whatever. She figured that if this was the way it was going to be, then Lou would have to live with the very rules that he made. She would see to that.

Cindy got her chance to give Lou a dose of his own medicine a few months later. A group of his best friends and their wives were planning to get together to play some miniature golf before going out to a new Indian restaurant that had gotten rave reviews. Lou was looking forward to it, and it would give everybody a chance to finally meet Cindy — or so he thought.

Cindy had other ideas. "I'm not going, Lou, but you go ahead and enjoy yourself."

Lou was practically sputtering. "Are you SERIOUS? These guys are my closest friends! We grew up together and their wives are great. You'll really like everybody. They're all looking forward to meeting you. We're going to have a wonderful time!"

"I TOLD you, Lou — I'm not going. I'm not a golfer and the thought of eating Indian food turns my stomach. Why would I want to get stuck doing something that I won't enjoy with a bunch of people I don't even know? Go without me and have a good time."

Lou tried to reason with her. "Cindy, it's going to be all couples. I'd feel like a fifth wheel, and besides, it wouldn't look right if I went without you."

"Oh, bullshit, Lou. If these people are such great friends of yours, you wouldn't feel out of place going out with them by yourself and they wouldn't be so quick to jump to conclusions, assuming that something is wrong between us just because I'm not there. Tell them that I already had other plans and was unable to join you. You're making a mountain out of a mole hill!"

"Judy and I were always doing things as a couple. Neither one of us would ever consider going to a couples oriented event without the other," Lou said.

That was all Cindy had to hear. "Dammit, Lou, I am NOT Judy and I am sick to death of you letting the terms of that marriage determine the rules of OUR relationship! You just don't want to take 'no' for an answer. You have no respect for my feelings. This is not something I would enjoy doing and I'm not going to tolerate an unbearable day of miniature golf followed by a meal with a bunch of strangers that I won't enjoy. I'm not going to put myself out that way just because JUDY did, and I'm sick and tired of you bringing her into the mix!"

Lou tried another approach. "It's all about making sacrifices, Cindy. This is what couples are supposed to do when they love each other. I guess it's just too much trouble for you, even though it would make me happy!"

"Really, Lou? Let's talk about making sacrifices! What about the time I asked you to go to Atlantic City for the weekend? You knew how much I wanted us to go but you refused because it's 'not your thing' and because you wouldn't go with Judy. Remember that?"

"Don't try to turn this around on me, Cindy. You know that I would have gone. It's not just about Judy; I didn't want to upset my kids."

"So, once again, I'm supposed to pay for something that happened between you and Judy? Why is this MY problem, and how many more times am I going to be at a disadvantage because of something that has to do with Judy? Let me tell you something, Lou. Judy may have begged you to go to Atlantic City, but I sure as hell won't beg. You made it clear that you didn't want to go to Atlantic City and I respected that. Now you're asking me to do something that I don't want to do. Like you, I am exercising my right to say no, so why won't you give me the same respect as I gave you and just accept my decision?"

"Aha, so now we're finally getting down to the ugly truth. You're playing tit for tat. I see what your game is!"

"It's no frigging game, Lou! You want me to 'yes' you all the time yet expect me to accept 'no' from you. Seems to me that you can't take what you dish out. I really and truly do NOT want to play miniature golf and I don't like Indian food, but you have to put an ugly spin on it because you're not getting your own way. It doesn't feel very good when the person you love disappoints you, does it? You expect me to suck it up when YOU can't even deal with it!"

Lou threw his hands up. "So plan a trip for us in Atlantic City, if that's what it'll take! If that's what I need to do to put an end to this nonsense, so be it. I give up. You win. Are you happy now?"

"Forget it, Lou. I don't want to go to Atlantic City with you if that's your attitude. I'll just go there with my friends. I don't have a problem with that. I wanted to go with YOU because I thought it would be nice for us to get away and do something together, but no, God forbid, it might upset your kids, and besides, you can't go to Atlantic City with me because you wouldn't go there with Judy. Well, I don't care what kind of crap Judy put up with; I expect a lot better for myself than what she was willing to settle for!"

Cindy was a real fireball. Lou loved and respected her independence and feisty spirit but sometimes it really got on his nerves. Although he might not admit it, Cindy made some very valid points.

We all learn from our mistakes. That's why people improve with age. Experience is the best teacher. Lou conceded that he should have gone to Atlantic City with Judy to make her happy, but then, hindsight is always 20/20. And now that Judy's dead, maybe he feels a sense of regret combined with some guilt about it, but that shouldn't have any impact on Cindy. The fact is that Lou does more to make Cindy happy than he ever did for Judy. While his concerns about upsetting his kids are valid, it's not Cindy's problem. Naturally, the kids will resent it if Lou goes to Atlantic City when he wouldn't go with their mother, but that should not be the deciding factor for what Lou does with Cindy.

Being with a widower is hard because it means stepping into a life that was designed by and for another woman. Habits and traditions have been formed, and the woman who comes after the late wife is expected to adapt, especially when a widower is still raising his kids. Certain sacrifices have to be made when you get into this kind of relationship, so the widower needs to be extra sensitive to the feelings of the next woman, even if it means upsetting his kids. They need to understand that their father is in love with her. When a man and woman are truly committed to each other, they are considered to be one and they must put each other first, above all others, including ex partners, late spouses, and kids.

The widower needs to set the tone. He must make his kids understand that this is a new day and the rules are different now. Nothing ever stays the same, and if a widower tries to shield his children from the harsh realities of life, he's only sparing them from learning how to cope with change and disappointment. But even more importantly, he is sending the message that the next woman in his life is Number Two and that sets her up for mistreatment and disrespect. Finally, his kids need to see that he has learned from his mistakes and is willing to change. Doing something for the new woman that he wouldn't do for the late wife indicates that he learned from the past and is trying to be a better man, and that's a GOOD thing.

17. MONEY

There are many reasons why your widower's children are resistant to their father getting remarried, and one of them may have to do with money. His kids are worried about who will get their inheritance. While the laws vary in different areas, in many cases the spouse is the automatic beneficiary by Right of Survivorship. Even if a former widower has a will that leaves his assets to his children, the local laws could overrule the will, granting everything to his surviving spouse unless she formally gives up her rights as the beneficiary.

When a couple marries and they have children from past relationships and marriages, it's always a good idea to have a financial plan in place ahead of time. This is especially important if there are vast economic differences between the two of them.

Let's take Irene, for example. She was an ambitious woman who worked hard and managed her finances well. She owned her own home outright. She budgeted her money carefully and made it a point to have regular monthly deposits put into her savings account to cushion her in case of some kind of emergency or setback. She brought her children up to be the same way. When she and Albert, a widower, became engaged, this was something that Irene wanted to address. For one thing, Albert made an excellent salary, but he spent money faster than he earned it. As a result, he was in a significant amount of debt and had no savings. Albert's adult children were the same way. They had an instant gratification mentality and spent money like there was no tomorrow. Albert's kids were rude, obnoxious, and disrespectful to Irene. They accused her of being a gold-digger who sold herself to the highest bidder and a lot of other things that I don't even want to mention. They made her feel unwelcome and awkward whenever she was in Albert's house.

When Albert proposed to Irene, true to form, her first thought was to work out all the financial arrangements before the wedding. The last thing Irene intended to do was to move into Albert's house, as it was the house he bought and lived in with his late wife. His kids made it clear that it was their mother's house. Irene knew that it would never feel like home to her. Albert agreed that it would be a problem for her to move in there, so it was decided that he would sell his house and move into hers. That, too, had the potential for trouble. In the event that Albert outlived Irene, he would inherit her house, her savings, her pension, etc. Irene couldn't stand seeing him and his kids getting everything that she wanted to leave to her own children, so they worked out a joint pre-nuptial agreement and updated their wills in ways that were mutually agreeable to both of them.

Just for the sake of argument, let's take a look at what could happen if Irene and Albert did not have a pre-nup or a will. Suppose there was an auto accident and Irene died instantly. Let's also say that Albert died the next day as the result of his injuries. Technically and legally speaking, when Irene died, Albert was alive and was, therefore, Irene's survivor at the time of her death, so he would be her beneficiary. Since he died the next day, however, his kids would be HIS beneficiary, and because he was widowed for the one day that he survived Irene, he would be legally entitled to everything she owned during the one day that he outlived her. When he died the next day, everything that he inherited from Irene would then be passed on to his kids, effectively cutting Irene's kids out of getting any of their mother's assets.

I know this is an extreme example, but even if a couple doesn't have any money at all, it's still a good idea to have a legal agreement in place to address any potential financial settlements in the event of an untimely or accidental death where a lawsuit might be involved.

Sam, a widower of very modest means, married Doris, a widow. Sam and Doris lived in a rented apartment, with no real savings and no other assets. They were retired with Social Security payments being their only source of income. They were both in relatively good health when Sam died as the result of a medical error. He was given the wrong medication during the course of a routine procedure and died from an allergic reaction to the drug. An attorney reached out to Doris and she filed a malpractice suit. It turned out to be an open and shut case, which was quickly settled out of court, providing Doris with a generous amount of money. Sam's children got wind of it and went after Doris for "their share." They ended up getting nothing, but it cost Doris a substantial amount of money in legal fees to defend herself against their claims to the money. If Sam had a will and/or there was a pre-nup, this battle could have been avoided, as his wishes would have been clearly defined and it would have spared Doris the stress of fighting a lawsuit with Sam's kids on top of her grief over his untimely death.

Money tends to be a touchy subject for a lot of people. Everything should be spelled out clearly before getting married; and this is especially important when you have children from past marriages or relationships. It wouldn't be an issue if your spouse was the parent of your children and vice versa, but since this wasn't the case with Irene and Albert or Sam and Doris, it would have been a good idea to sit down and get these issues settled before getting married so that there wouldn't be any legal battles later on, should money be involved when one or both spouses pass away.

These are matters that should be between the marrying couple only. They don't need the approval or permission of their children. Furthermore, the kids shouldn't even be told about any agreements because it could only lead to arguments. This is one area where it's best to keep certain details of your lives between yourselves — especially if you're marrying a widower.

18. DOUBLE STANDARDS

Rosie had been seeing Jay, a widower to whom she had recently become engaged. They went out to dinner with several couples who had known Jay and his late wife for years. This was a tight-knit group of friends with a long history together. Naturally, Rosie felt awkward because these people were all familiar with each other while she, a complete stranger, had never met any of them. In their effort to make Rosie feel included, someone would explain the meaning behind all the private jokes and laughs the group enjoyed. Naturally, the reminiscing began. Rosie was listening to all the memories they shared and then out came the photos of holidays, vacations, and other celebrations, which included Jay and Wanda, his late wife. Rosie sat there uncomfortably as she had to look at one picture after another until she was ready to scream.

In the car on the way home, she was in tears. "I never felt so out of place in my entire life!" she said to Jay.

"Why?" he wanted to know.

"Why the hell do you think? I was treated like an outsider! I realize that I'm a stranger to your friends, but did they have to make it so obvious?"

Jay didn't get it. "They were trying to be nice to you. They were only trying to share our history with you so you wouldn't feel left out."

"THAT was their way of trying to make me feel included? By talking about Wanda, reminiscing about all fun they had with her and passing around photos of their happy memories with the two of you? If that was their way of making me feel welcome, thank God they weren't trying to treat me like an outsider!"

"Well, what else did you expect them to talk about? We've all been friends for years. Should they pretend that Wanda never existed? Wanda was a part of all those memories. They accept that Wanda is gone and they're trying to be friendly toward you. It was awkward for THEM, too!"

Rosie was hurt that he could not or would not try to see her side of the situation. "It was a lot less awkward for them, because they had each other for support. I had nobody on my side!"

Jay was clueless. "Rosie, there ARE no sides! It was just a group of our friends trying to get to know you."

Rosie was upset that he referred to them as "our friends," meaning his and Wanda's. He and Wanda were still "we," and that stung.

Rosie came to me for my opinion and I offered her several suggestions. "If you're going to be thrown together with these people on a regular basis, it should be at sporting events, concerts, movies, day trips, or other activities where you won't have to do much talking. This way, you'll be enjoying yourself and making your OWN memories with this group and then later on, when you ARE out to dinner or other social situations with them, your picture will be included among the photos and you'll be able to participate in the conversations. Another option is to avoid all interaction with these couples if they make you feel like an outsider. However, if their intentions are sincere and they are genuinely trying to be nice, it might be worth it to stick it out until they get to know you better. It would also be a good idea to try to develop friendships with new couples who have no history with either of you."

Rosie's frustrations were certainly understandable and definitely justifiable. For some reason, people seem to think it's okay to talk about a late wife in front of the new woman in the widower's life. Nobody considers that it would bother her. They just cannot understand why she would have a problem with it. On the other hand, if a man were DIVORCED, the rules would be different. People wouldn't even consider talking about their happy memories of the ex-wife or passing around her photos. Marriages and relationships that end by the death of a partner are not subject to the same unspoken terms and conditions that apply to couples who have broken up. This is a terrible double standard and unless somebody has been in such a situation, they don't usually get it.

I would love to know how these same couples would have reacted if Rosie started talking about one of her former lovers or her ex-husband, complete with photos and emotional comments about how great they were as a couple, all the wonderful times they had together, and how much she missed him. My guess is that they'd be appalled and even angry that she had the nerve to say such things now that she was seriously involved with their widowed friend. They would assume that Rosie was with Jay on the rebound, yet they would expect HER to overlook this same behavior when the focus was on Jay's late wife.

Without a doubt, it is awkward to sit there among people you hardly know who all share a history with each other and listen while they recall times in their lives that did not include you. They were at each other's weddings, funerals of relatives, they were there for the birth of each other's children, they've taken trips together, and there were several other events, holidays, and functions they shared with your widower and his late wife. You may even experience hostility and rejection from some of the wives because you could be a threat to them. Your presence might cause them to secretly fear that their own husbands would easily replace them with another woman if they were to pass away. Maybe they're worried that their husbands envy that happy glow on your widower's face these days. After all, he's getting another chance with a fresh new love. After seeing him so lost and broken up after the death of his late wife, there is suddenly a bounce in his step, a warm glow of happiness on his face, and a twinkle in his eyes. There's nothing like the thrill of an exciting new romance, and this can cause their own marriages to feel stale and monotonous by comparison.

Whatever the reason is, it's never okay for your widower or anyone in his life to babble on and on about the late wife in your company. She's gone. She's never coming back. She's out of the picture forever. No matter what the situation, it's rude and inconsiderate to talk about a previous relationship to the current woman. Just for the sake of comparison, let's reverse the situation. Say that you and your widower go out with several couples who used to socialize with you and your former husband or ex-boyfriend. Now imagine that they all sit around, laughing as they recall funny situations, private jokes, memories and experiences that they shared with you and your ex. On and on they go, swapping anecdotes and passing around photos of themselves with the two of you while your widower sits there like a bump on a log, feeling like an idiot while listening to all this nonsense. Would he be offended and irritated? Yes, without a doubt! He would consider their actions to be rude and ill-mannered, yet nobody seems to think there's anything wrong with this same behavior if the former spouse or partner is deceased. Widowers aren't exempt from the courtesy that you would expect from any other man. They don't get a free pass just because they lost their wives. Everybody experiences pain and loss during the course of their lives. A widower's grief is no worse than anybody else's. It's not a license for people to do whatever they want.

Suppose you went on and on to your widower about a former love, lamenting that your time together was cut short because the relationship didn't work out. Imagine how it would make him feel to listen to your mournful saga about how much you miss another guy, and that you'll always love him and keep him in your heart. His first thought would be that you're on the rebound, using him as a shock absorber for your heartache. He would think that you're really not yet ready to be in another relationship, and he would be right. Funny how it's not acceptable to act that way over an ex, yet it's perfectly suitable if the former spouse or partner has died. A definite and glaringly blatant double standard!

19. MEMORIAL EVENTS

Whether it's his doing or not, some widowers will support or participate in memorial events in their late wife's memory. This is a situation that can be emotionally devastating to the woman who loves a widower.

Tracy's husband was a former widower. Her husband Drew met Kathy, his late wife, when they were in high school. They had been married for nearly thirty years when Kathy died of breast cancer. For a while, Drew expected his late wife to beat this disease. Kathy fought for several years, having many good periods of remission and indications that she would survive her illness, but ultimately it got the better of her.

When Kathy was first diagnosed, Drew and Kathy's three children became involved with an annual fundraising walk/race to raise money for research and to create more awareness about breast cancer. Without a doubt, it's a worthy cause. Tracy understood and respected that. What she DIDN'T like was the way they went about it. Each year, the three children organized their own memorial group, "Team Kathy," in honor of their late mother. This team would participate in the annual walk/race wearing pink t-shirts and carrying banners bearing Kathy's photo and the date of her death. After the race was over, the group had a tradition of releasing dozens of pink balloons in Kathy's memory. Drew was active in this annual event, much to Tracy's disapproval. Drew was HER husband now and it humiliated her that he dedicated his time and energy to the memory of another woman. He promoted "Team Kathy" heavily on social media and urged his friends, family, co-workers, former in-laws, and neighbors to attend the race, rain or shine.

Drew and Tracy's wedding anniversary was in October, which also happens to be Breast Cancer Awareness Month. He continued to participate in the race and wore something pink all month in honor of breast cancer awareness. This caused many arguments between Drew and Tracy. She felt that he should end his involvement with this event and should certainly not promote it any longer. Drew disagreed, arguing that he was supporting his children's efforts and that it was a worthy cause that benefits EVERYONE. Tracy did not argue with that; her problem was that the focus was on KATHY, not on the overall fundraising organization. She felt strongly that her feelings were valid and quite justified.

By the time Tracy came to me with this problem, she and Drew had been married for three years and there was no indication that the problem would be going away any time soon. There could be a fair compromise if she and Drew were both willing to bend. This fundraiser IS a worthy cause. Nobody can deny that. The fact is, however, that Kathy was neither the first woman to die of breast cancer, nor would she be the last. My suggestion was for Drew to keep his focus on his wedding anniversary to Tracy during the month of October. He needed to stop wearing pink and to back away from the activities organized in Kathy's memory. His three children were adults. They could promote "Team Kathy" among their own friends, neighbors, co-workers, and their late mother's side of the family. There was nothing wrong with Drew wanting to support this valuable fundraiser, but he could do so by making a generous contribution to the organization without any reference to Kathy's memory. He did not need to include her in the equation or participate in the event in order to continue supporting the cause.

When Tracy tried to explain this to Drew, he complained that it was only taking up a few hours out of one day a year. This wasn't true. There was about a month's worth of preparation and planning that went into what Drew referred to as an annual few-hour event. Pink t-shirts and banners needed to be designed that featured a different photo of Kathy each year. Research had to be done to find a company that would turn out the best quality of these items for the lowest price. Then there were the Facebook promotions and postings, urging and encouraging people to participate and donate to this great cause "in honor of Kathy's memory." All the time and effort amounted to multiple days over the course of each year. Tracy couldn't stand it, but Drew just blew her off, accusing her of trying to discourage him from supporting his kids.

When Drew chose to get involved with Tracy and then marry her, his actions were an indication that he was letting go of Kathy and starting a whole new life with someone new. He did not and could not understand Tracy's humiliation when her friends, family, and co-workers would see him promoting the memory of his late wife. What he was doing, in effect, was making a public announcement that he was still thinking about another woman. This was an embarrassing slap in the face to Tracy, whose entire heart and soul belonged to Drew and ONLY Drew.

Drew insisted that he loved Tracy with all of his heart and that he couldn't be happier; however, he didn't realize how it looked to other people when he pranced around in pink during the month of October promoting "Team Kathy" or the pain and embarrassment it caused Tracy. He couldn't understand why she had a problem with it. In HIS mind, she was asking him to dismiss the memory of a person who had been a part of his life for over thirty years, even though those thirty years were over. He had no further obligation to Kathy. He had completely satisfied his responsibilities to that marriage. The vows are "til death do us part." He needed to let go in order to focus on his marriage to Tracy, giving her the same full level of commitment he had given to his previous marriage. Kathy never had to deal with the frustration of another woman's spirit invading her marriage; Tracy was entitled to nothing less.

Drew felt like he would be abandoning his children if he cut himself off from the annual race. He didn't think they'd understand why he would instead give a generous donation but back out of all the activities. It seemed that Drew was more concerned about upsetting his children than hurting Tracy's feelings. Both felt that the other was being unreasonable. This ongoing problem became progressively worse…neither Drew nor Tracy would budge. In Drew's mind, it was non-negotiable; in Tracy's mind, it was intolerable. What happened is that Tracy began emotionally withdrawing from Drew. At first, she would stay upset for a few weeks, but in time she gave up trying to reason with him after it became obvious that his position wasn't going to change. As time went on, her feelings for him began to diminish. A wall began to develop inside of her, a sort of defense mechanism to protect her feelings and her heart. Tracy had been hurt before but never in this way. As time went on, she became more and more detached and apathetic. She didn't even bother to argue with Drew anymore, realizing that it would serve absolutely no purpose. She still cared for him, but the intensity of her feelings dissipated. Her love for him was slowly diminishing and Drew felt the disconnection. He couldn't put his finger on what was wrong or what was happening because they seemed to be getting along fairly well most of the time. What he didn't realize was that Tracy was tired of arguing over a situation with no end in sight. She basically gave up trying to fight this losing battle, but it was often on her mind as a constant thorn in her side until their "relationship" was all on the surface.

They went on this way for another few years until she finally told him that their marriage was no longer working for her and that she thought it would be best if they went their separate ways. Drew was angry and baffled. He thought everything was fine, but it wasn't. They weren't arguing about it anymore simply because Tracy had stopped caring.

Drew was furious, demanding to know what was REALLY going on.

Did she meet another man? Was she being spiteful? What the hell was her problem?

She told him that they just didn't see eye to eye on certain things and didn't think they ever would. She reminded him about how upsetting it was for her to see him actively involved in the walk/race in Kathy's memory every year. True to form, Drew accused her of being "ridiculous, over-reacting, and being a control freak." He ridiculed, belittled, minimized and dismissed her feelings as being silly and trivial. He insisted that Tracy was only using this as an excuse to end the marriage. What Tracy heard was that her feelings were not that significant and that the annual event in his late wife's memory was far more important to Drew than staying married to her. The bottom line was that it no longer mattered to Tracy. She was tired of fighting for the portion of Drew's heart that he wouldn't give her. She didn't feel that she should HAVE to work so hard for the rightful place that any other wife should expect to have in her husband's life.

At that point, Drew suggested marriage counseling, but Tracy firmly told him that there wasn't a therapist in the world who could convince her to overlook this unbearable situation. To her, it was a deal breaker. She told Drew that maybe HE should seek counseling to find a way to break his ties to the past or to find a woman who thought so little of herself that she was willing to accept second place.

There were no winners in this Mexican standoff. Tracy and Drew ended up selling the home they bought together when they married. They split the money from the sale of the house and quietly parted ways. It was not a bitter, ugly, bloodbath divorce. It was simply the tired resignation of two people who could not find an acceptable middle ground between their differences. This way, Drew could spend the rest of his life supporting the memory of his late wife if that's what he needed to do, and Tracy could either enjoy a peaceful, single existence or find someone else who was one hundred percent on board with her and ONLY her.

20. THE "THREE HEARTS PHILOSOPHY"

This is one of the most controversial subjects I have ever encountered during my research into relationships with widowers. There are two powerful, opposing forces who vehemently disagree about this and, as a result, there is a huge division between the people on both sides of this debate.

The "Three Hearts Philosophy," which is at the very core of this book and illustrated on the cover, supports the belief that there can be three people in a relationship: the widower, the current woman in his life, and the late wife. Strong arguments continue to rage about this sensitive subject in an ongoing social media battlefield with no end in sight.

On one side of the argument are the women who condone and promote the late wife's memory. They exercise "patience, compassion, and support" for their widower's ongoing grief and attachment to the late wife. They have contempt for those who are intolerant of the three-hearts relationship, criticizing them for their insensitivity, selfishness, and lack of consideration for the man they love. They claim that the woman who does not support the memory of her man's late wife is selfish and insecure.

A woman who sees herself as there to support the widower through his mourning for his late wife is pretty much assuming the role of therapist/social worker, and yet she is having sex with him. There is something distasteful about that. It's as if the female therapist happily compromises her integrity by sleeping with the guy she is trying to help. It's a conflict of interest, and the woman is just as bad for hanging around waiting until a widower is ready to give all of his heart to her, instead of using her as an emotional crutch and sex buddy.

So what exactly does it mean to embrace the "three hearts" mindset? Terry is a perfect example. She was always the kind of person who loved taking care of others, whether it was an injured animal, or a person who was ill or just down on his or her luck. She was a master champion for the underdog and nothing gave her more pleasure or satisfaction than to help somebody in any kind of distress. Not surprisingly, she had a career as a nurse and one of her patients was Nicole, a woman dying of a severe kidney disease.

Terry was, hands down, everyone's favorite nurse. She became friends with Nicole's husband, Pete, a regular visitor who spent every possible minute with Nicole at the hospital. Pete was deeply grateful to Terry for taking such good care of Nicole and keeping her comfortable, often going above and beyond the call of duty to do so. Terry was right there by Pete's side when Nicole took her final breath and held him as he sobbed by her bedside. Terry attended the funeral and afterwards sent Pete a sympathy card along with her telephone number and a handwritten note to call her any time he needed a shoulder to cry on. She even stopped by Pete's house on her time off on a few occasions to check in on him and to see how he was holding up. As somebody who was very familiar with Nicole's final struggle, Pete could think of no one better than Terry to call upon whenever he was overwhelmed with grief. They quickly transitioned from friendship to intimacy, with Terry moving into Pete's house only six months after Nicole died.

Terry took care of all the household chores, as well as Pete and Nicole's three children, who were all under the age of ten. On the day of what would have been Nicole's birthday, Terry threw a party and presented Pete and the kids with a beautiful scrapbook containing photos, poems, and other sentimental tokens of Nicole's memory. She went out of her way to comfort Pete and the kids on all of the other "firsts" without Nicole: the date of what would have been their wedding anniversary, Valentine's Day, Mother's Day, Thanksgiving, etc. Terry made it a point to include Nicole in as much of their lives as possible. She took flowers to Nicole's grave and held Pete as he cried over her headstone. She had Christmas ornaments made with Nicole's picture on them and adorned the house with Nicole's decorations. Her Christmas gift to Pete and the kids was a digital photo album that displayed a large variety of pictures taken with and of Nicole during the course of their lives with her. Terry maintained all Nicole's holiday traditions. Pete was pleased. It meant that he could hang on to his beloved Nicole, even though her physical presence was gone. During a particularly emotional moment, Terry held Pete as he sobbed, telling him that if she could bring Nicole back to him, she would. She promised to do everything in her power to keep Nicole's memory alive for him and the children. At the same time, she made a conscious effort to stay in the background for Pete and the children so that their focus could stay on Nicole.

Terry was proud of her nurturing instincts. As an active Facebook user, she eagerly shared her "wisdom" with several groups designed to support those facing challenges in their relationships with widowers, and oh, how the floodgates opened! A small number of the groups' members admired Terry for her sensitivity, and the "strength" not to feel threatened by Pete's love and ongoing attachment to Nicole. They applauded Terry's ability to rise above petty jealousy by including Nicole in her life.

The majority of people, however, ripped Terry to shreds. They called Terry a doormat and complained that it was women like her who made things so difficult for women who had too much self-respect to settle for a man who couldn't give his all in a relationship. Terry shot back, accusing them of being hateful, heartless, narrow-minded, and lacking confidence for feeling "intimidated" by the late wife.

The vicious backlash continued as the opposing members told Terry that a dead woman couldn't "return" due to the fact that she was never truly gone. Terry made sure of that. They insisted that Terry was so insecure that she would settle for crumbs rather than go without a man. They emphasized the fact that Terry's actions encouraged Pete and the children to stay mired in their grief and prevented them from moving on. They warned Terry that Pete could never be able see her as anything more than an extension of Nicole and that he would never love her for herself. They asked her if she was willing to settle for only being loved for how much of Nicole's spirit she could keep alive for them.

Those in Terry's corner came back at her critics by accusing them of being petty, vicious, and self-centered, arguing that it's because of Terry's unconditional love and support that Pete cares about her so much. They argued that Pete, or any other grieving widower, has just as much right to be in a relationship as anyone else and that he should not be expected to subject himself to loneliness just because he is still attached to his late wife.

Those who supported the three hearts mentality were in the minority. The greatest number of people in the various groups were all about moving on, second chances, living in the present, refusing to settle for only a portion of a person's heart, and choosing to end the relationship if they weren't treated as a priority.

Some women feel the need to embroil and entrench themselves in the family's grief for the lost woman. It never ceases to amaze me that some women can assume that this is their role, yet many didn't even know the dead woman. I put it down to insecurity — almost as if the women with the three hearts mentality are trying to intertwine themselves with the widower's history to more firmly root themselves in his life. All this does is limit their ability to be anything more to the man whom they love than someone who can keep the late wife's essence alive.

Three Hearts Supporters = low self-esteem, fear of being alone, willingness to settle, and justification for their actions.

Anti-Three Hearts Supporters = confidence, courage, self-respect, unwillingness to settle, strength to walk away, ability to be alone, make no apologies for setting boundaries, and holding out for a man who makes her his Number One.

I have done my best to present fair and unbiased consideration for both sides of these types of relationships, but I make no secret as to where I stand regarding my own personal views. While I always made it a point not to engage in any nasty online arguments, that never stopped me from openly expressing my own opinions. I firmly believe that it is DEAD WRONG (no pun intended) for a widower to pass himself off as "available" just because he is technically and legally unmarried. If he is still grieving or has an emotional attachment to any part of his late wife, he should refrain from getting involved in another relationship because he is leading an innocent woman on under false pretenses. The truth is that such men are NOT "available" if they can only be there physically but not emotionally. It's far better for a widower to fully recover and put the past behind him to better his chances of finding a QUALITY relationship and falling in love again. If a still-grieving widower finds someone who will accept what little he has to offer, he needs to question the value of a woman who is willing to settle for a man who can only offer a warm body and little else.

There have been a small number of the three heart supporters who have attacked my beliefs, but I have simply let them have their say and have not responded. An argument is a dance that requires two partners, and I am not willing to get drawn into this senseless debate. I am never going to change my position on this, and I will not waste my valuable time going back and forth with an opponent. I refuse to explain, defend, excuse, or justify my opinion. My attitude is: Take what you like and leave the rest.

If you want a meaningful relationship with a truly available man, you should NEVER get involved with a grief-stricken widower. To do so is to set yourself up to be used to fill whatever void there is in his life while your own needs go unmet. You will continually be disappointed when he fails to live up to your expectations of enjoying a normal, healthy relationship. Grieving is not a couple's activity. The late wife is not part of YOUR memories and her passing is not YOUR loss, just like YOUR former relationships are not your partner's memory to embrace. You would never expect him to go along for the ride while you cry over the end of a previous relationship. He should not expect anything different from you. Make sure that the late wife is completely out of his system before letting a relationship with a widower go any further. He needs to be SO over her if he wants a place in your life. He shouldn't be able to ride two horses with one ass.

You do NOT want to be a crying towel. You do NOT want to be a grief counselor. You do NOT want to be a placeholder. You do NOT want to be the rebound woman. You do NOT want to be treated like Plan B. You do NOT want to be used as a shock absorber for his pain. You do NOT want to feel like a consolation prize. You are NOT a buffer for his loss. You are NOT his second choice.

If your widower's children are old enough to remember the late wife, they'll never let you forget that you are NOT their mother, yet you'll be expected to accept all the responsibilities that used to be hers. For those of you whose widowers have very young children, you will be the only mother they ever know, but that won't stop the late wife's family from trying to push her memory on to them. If the children want to hang on to their mother's memory, they should ABSOLUTELY feel free to do so — she WAS their mother, after all. The point is that the late wife's relatives should not force their own grief on the children or make them feel guilty for loving you as their stepmother.

As the woman of the house, you need to set strong boundaries for the children. It's a delicate situation because your presence is a painful reminder that their loved one is gone forever, so you cannot be without kindness and sensitivity, but not to the point where you're treated like an unwelcome intruder or your authority is undermined. It is very important for you and your widower to present a united front in this situation so that his former in-laws cannot play one of you against the other. This is the only kind of relationship where you are expected to include another woman's family into your life and it can be very emotionally draining at times.

If the children are adults, they can spend time with their mother's relatives on their own, but if they're young, this is something that you sign up for when you marry a widower who is still raising his children. It's not a situation that anybody would choose to be in, but you need to try to make it as comfortable as possible for all concerned without becoming a three hearts champion or diminishing yourself in the process. It's a tough balancing act that not many woman can handle, myself included.

21. CEMETERY/BURIAL ARRANGEMENTS

Jocelyn was a young widow who was only married for two years when her husband Ted drowned. She grieved for a couple of years but finally decided that it was time for her to be happy and start living again. While her memories of Ted were pleasant, they had long since faded into the background as she got more and more caught up in her present-day life. She dated and was involved in different relationships over the years that, for various reasons, did not work out. She was especially weary of the headaches and drama that came with men who were divorced, so when she met Ralph, a nice widower, she was elated. There would be no one to take a portion of his pension, no bratty kids to play one parent against the other, and no arguments as to who would get the kids over the holidays. At fifty-five, Ralph was about ten years older than Jocelyn and by the time she met him, his four kids were grown and on their own. In Jocelyn's mind, this was an ideal situation. There would be no bitter ex-wives in the picture, no alimony or child support payments, and no stepchildren to take care of. She figured that she and Ralph would be free to do whatever they wanted and, for the most part, she was right.

Ralph wasn't the typical grieving widower. He and his late wife had a reasonably happy marriage with the usual ups and downs. Jeanette had a bad heart for most of her life and was in and out of the hospital many times over the years. Her health got progressively worse over time. She and Ralph both knew that it would eventually get the better of her, so her death came as no surprise. He had no false hopes for any miracles and had long since come to terms with the inevitable. Fortunately, Ralph had a chance to tell Jeanette all the things he wanted to say to her as she hovered between life and death. Before she slipped into a final coma, Jeanette told Ralph that she loved him, appreciated his patience and care for her throughout her long illness, thanked him for all the happy years of marriage he gave her, asked him to remember her fondly without dwelling on her, and made him promise to be happy and find love again. It sounded too good to be true, right? It did and it was.

Jocelyn had heard horror stories from Sue, one of her best friends who married Joe, a former widower. Sue cautioned Jocelyn to tread carefully with Ralph, warning her that widowers come with a whole different set of problems that she wouldn't be expecting. Jocelyn thanked Sue for her concern, explaining that Ralph's situation was different from Joe's. Ralph already did all his grieving during the many years that Jeanette's health continued to deteriorate. Ralph was a good husband, and therefore had no associated guilt or sense of obligation to keep Jeanette's memory alive. He already got the closure he needed. His kids were okay with him dating and they were actually happy for their father and Jocelyn when they got engaged. Jocelyn insisted to Sue that everything would be hunky-dory. For the most part, Jocelyn was right, but as Sue warned her, over time, situations began to come up that she hadn't been expecting.

The first Christmas after she and Ralph got engaged, she went with him to place a wreath on Jeanette's grave. Jocelyn figured that it was Ralph's way of saying his final goodbyes before moving ahead in his life with her. The earliest sign of trouble began when she found out that Ralph continued to make occasional trips to the cemetery. In the beginning, Jocelyn let it go, figuring that this was a habit that would fade out over time. After they had been together for a couple of years, however, Ralph continued to go to the cemetery every once in a while so Jocelyn finally decided that it was time to talk to him about it. He was genuinely baffled by her objections.

"Why do you have a problem with this? I'm not taking anything away from you, and I'm only at Jeanette's grave for about ten minutes," he argued.

"It's not about the ten minutes," Jocelyn said. "It's about the fact that Jeanette is on your mind enough for you to take time out of your day to make the thirty minute drive to the cemetery to visit her grave. You ARE, in fact, taking something away from me because a part of you is still tied to the past. It tells me that your mind and heart are divided between Jeanette and me. She didn't have to share your thoughts or time and attention with another woman, so why should I?"

Ralph didn't get it. "She's DEAD, Jocelyn, so you're not sharing ANYTHING with Jeanette. I'm simply taking a little time out of my life to honor her memory out of respect for the years we shared together. I have long since gotten over her passing. I'm ten years older than you and chances are that you'll outlive me, so after I'm gone, I'd like to think that you'll want to make occasional trips there yourself."

Jocelyn just about lost it. "What are you saying, Ralph? Are you telling me that you're planning to be buried with Jeanette?"

"Yes, I am. This was something that Jeanette and I planned together a long time ago. I thought you knew that!"

"No, Ralph, I did NOT know that! How would I? You never mentioned it to me before, because if you did, it's not something that I would have forgotten! What on Earth could have possessed you to do such a stupid thing? What in God's name could you have been thinking? You knew that Jeanette was dying. Didn't it ever occur to you that you'd get remarried and that it would be a mistake to make that kind of commitment to your previous spouse?"

"I'm not committed to her, Jocelyn. They're just burial plans! What difference is it going to make? We'll be dead! It's not like we're going to be getting it on in the grave! It's not MY fault that you didn't make burial plans of your own. If you had made similar arrangements with your late husband, I wouldn't have a problem with it."

"Ralph, for one thing, Ted and I were only married for two years. I never expected him to drown. I never thought he'd die that young, but even if I did, I would NEVER have made burial plans that early in life, knowing that I might be married to somebody else later on. What if I married another guy and had children with him a few years later? Don't you think it would be upsetting to my husband and kids for me to be buried with a man they never knew? How do you think it's going to make ME feel to see my husband buried with some other woman, a complete stranger to me?"

Ralph really and truly didn't get it. He felt that it was "only right" for his kids to have their parents buried together. While that might sound logical, it was still hurtful to Jocelyn and made her feel like an outsider in Ralph's family unit. What Ralph was telling Jocelyn, in effect, was that Jeanette was the REAL wife, his MAIN spouse. SHE was the one he made a family with. It made Jocelyn feel secondary and inferior, like THIS marriage was less significant because they weren't bonded together by children and had no shared history. Her friend Sue was right. Jocelyn would never have to deal with this problem if she was engaged to a man who was divorced. Not only did Ralph continue to visit his late wife's grave, he was going to be buried there with her someday. If that wasn't bad enough, Ralph's response just about blew her away after she insisted how unfair it was to her.

"Jocelyn, you and I didn't get together until I was more than halfway through my life; therefore, you are owed something different than the woman who was there with me from the beginning," Ralph said.

Jocelyn nearly lost her mind when she heard that. "Is that right, Ralph? So, I am owed 'something different' because I came into the picture later in life? If you ask ME, I should be owed MORE than Jeanette because I'll have to put up with things that Jeanette never had to deal with; for example, the effects of time. You'll slow down with age and be less able to do as much when you get older. I will be the one, not Jeanette, who will be taking care of you in your golden years, through sickness and other problems that arise over the course of time. She had your energy and your youth. I'm getting your baggage and the aches and pains of old age!"

"That's what marriage is all about, Jocelyn! We took vows for better or worse, in sickness and in health! I honored that commitment with Jeanette and I would do nothing less for you!" Ralph shot back.

"Since we're talking about vows, what about the part about forsaking all others, being faithful only to each other?" Jocelyn asked him.

"I AM and will CONTINUE be faithful to you and ONLY you!" Ralph told her. "Why are you making such a big deal out of my occasional trips to the cemetery and about my burial plans with Jeanette? The vows are only good until death do us part, so when I die, my obligation to you is finished."

"Really, Ralph? If your obligation to a spouse is finished after death do us part, then why are you still honoring the vows you made with Jeanette? According to what you just said, your obligation to her is finished. Furthermore, by forsaking all others and being faithful only to me, that doesn't just mean to do so only in a sexual or romantic sense. Fidelity comes in many forms. It includes an emotional and relational intimacy — a full, one hundred percent commitment to me and ONLY me! I deserve nothing less than what you gave to Jeanette and what ANY married woman has a right to expect!"

As Jocelyn correctly pointed out, there's another form of being unfaithful that isn't about romance or sex; it's about the emotional and relational connection. The reality is that if you are closer to anyone other than your spouse, you are being disloyal to your marriage vows. The object of your affection could even be a child, a parent, a best friend, or a hobby. If there is an investment in anyone or anything that takes precedence over your relationship with your spouse, it crosses the line into betrayal.

In Ralph's mind, one marriage has nothing to do with the other, and one of the consequences of getting remarried later in life is that a part of the past will come into the picture from time to time. As far as he is concerned, his burial plans with Jeanette are non-negotiable, and he told Jocelyn that he did not intend to change them, that it was not an option.

This is what is considered to be a Hobson's Choice; in other words, take it or leave it. Ralph and Jocelyn are at opposite ends of the spectrum in their views about this situation and there's no acceptable middle ground to be found here. What should be done about this type of dilemma? Do you throw out all of the good in a relationship to get rid of the one or two bad things? Doesn't every couple in the world have to face their own set of challenges? If Jocelyn looks the other way when it comes to the cemetery visits and Ralph's burial arrangements, is she sending him the message that she'll continue to accept things that she considers to be intolerable? Will she be setting a dangerous precedent for future conflicts? Where should her boundaries begin and end? At what point does it cross the line?

This was no easy decision. Ralph was taking the risk of losing Jocelyn over a dead woman. Jocelyn was taking the risk of throwing away a good man solely on principle. In my opinion, this is a classic case of a Catch-22 situation.

I can certainly understand Ralph's point about his kids having their parents buried together. People make these types of decisions based on their current reality. They never stop to wonder if they'll ever marry again, if the next spouse may have any objections, or whether that person, too, has their own pre-planned burial arrangements already in place.

Jocelyn's feelings are equally valid; she wants no less than what ANY wife should rightfully expect. It's not HER fault that her young husband died suddenly and tragically. She shouldn't be denied the options that Jeanette had with Ralph simply because she happened to come into his life in his later years. Jocelyn didn't want her marriage to Ralph to be influenced by Jeanette's spirit in any way, shape, or form. It's not the person you start out with but the one you end up with who should matter the most.

Some people considered Jocelyn's dilemma with Ralph to be a deal breaker. Others felt that Jocelyn should just let it go, considering that this was her only real fly in the ointment. She could certainly do a lot worse. Ralph is a good, solid husband; he's a one-woman man who treats Jocelyn with kindness, respect, and consideration. And let's face it, EVERYBODY who marries later in life gets hit with occasional remnants of the past in one form or another. It all boils down to what is acceptable to the couple involved, based on their mindset and level of tolerance.

Jocelyn felt that Ralph's trips to the cemetery were comparable to her visiting an ex-boyfriend. She made it clear that she wouldn't tell him not to go there, but Ralph knew that it would only create resentment in Jocelyn. He knew her well enough to realize that the anger would fester inside her and her feelings for him would slowly wane until the relationship became little more than a shell. Jocelyn believed in total unity in a relationship and any ongoing attachment to a former lover or spouse, dead or alive, wouldn't sit well with her. Ralph loved Jocelyn and didn't want to lose her over something like this. His obligation to Jeanette was fully satisfied and that marriage was over. He needed to let Jeanette go, stop the graveside visits at the cemetery and give Jocelyn his all; he felt that this was a fair compromise, since he didn't want to budge on the burial plans.

I have to give Jocelyn a lot of credit for her ingenuity. She came up with a very interesting and unique way to level the playing field. She went ahead and married Ralph in spite of the fact that they were never able to resolve these differences before the wedding, but instead of taking Ralph's last name, she decided to keep the last name she already had, which was the last name of her late husband. Ralph didn't like that one bit, but Jocelyn told him that she would be keeping Ted's name unless Ralph removed HIS name from Jeanette's headstone. Quid pro quo.

22. FORMER IN-LAWS

If you ever saw the movie *Psycho In-Law*, you'll know exactly what this chapter is about. The movie is about the life of a widower and his young daughter after his late wife passes away. His former mother-in-law was unbearably meddlesome, and it gets a million times worse when his fiancée moves into the house. The young woman does a great job bonding with her future stepdaughter and they got along great. This doesn't sit well with the late wife's mother. She does everything in her power to sabotage her former son-in-law's relationship with his fiancée. The evil grandmother also tries to turn the child against her future stepmom. This fictional movie is an extreme example, but the basic storyline is actually a common scenario.

I'll tell you about one such situation. Brooke recently married Matt, a former widower with a young son and daughter. Matt's late wife, Rachel, committed suicide a few years earlier without warning or notice. She simply waited until Matt went to work and the kids were in school, then took an overdose of pills, went to bed, and never woke up. She didn't leave a note and there had been no indication that she would ever do anything like this. Rachel's mother, Gloria, was the one who found her. Gloria had always been a domineering, meddling, controlling type of person, and her daughter's suicide didn't change that. At first, she was a godsend to Matt, coming over to look after the kids after school while Matt was working, and she would often clean the house and get dinner started. She still had her house key and used it to let herself in every day.

Matt began dating a sweet woman named Brooke. One evening, after seeing each other for a few months, Brooke was over at the house spending time with Matt and the kids when Gloria walked in unannounced, explaining that she noticed a "strange car" in the driveway and wanted to make sure that "everything was okay." Matt introduced Brooke, explaining that she was his girlfriend. Gloria pasted a forced smile on her face, telling Brooke that it was nice to meet her. The two women were pleasant, but the tension in the air was unmistakable. Being satisfied that nothing was amiss, Gloria said her goodbyes and left.

During the next several months, Gloria continued to let herself in the house to look after Bobby and Kristin and noticed that the children were talking about Brooke constantly. She was very good to the children and they absolutely adored her. One day, when Grandma Gloria came by, Bobby, age eight, and Kristin, age six, excitedly told her that they were getting a new mom because Brooke would be moving in soon and she and Daddy were getting married.

Brooke was clearly aware that her presence was upsetting to Gloria, but she made her best effort to exercise patience and self-control with the older woman. Brooke kept in mind that Gloria had lost her only daughter and that her grandchildren were everything to her, so Brooke tried her best to be kind and compassionate toward Gloria, hoping that she would adapt and not feel threatened by the marriage. It got to the point, however, where Gloria took far too many liberties. She would often talk about Rachel, reminding the kids not to forget their mother, and would warn them to be careful not to get too attached to Brooke because she wasn't their "real" mother and would someday have very little time for them once she had children of her own.

One day Gloria walked in and started in on Brooke as she was making dinner, criticizing the meal she was preparing and offering to show her how to make it "the right way."

By this time, Brooke's patience was wearing thin, but she kept her composure as she tried to take charge of the situation. "Gloria, you've been a godsend to Matt and the children; I don't know how they would have managed without you all this time, but it's not fair for you to have all this responsibility. Now that I'm here, you don't have to do so much anymore. This will give you more time to spend on yourself and to enjoy the children instead of having to take care of them."

"Nonsense, my dear. I love my grandchildren and enjoy taking care of them and my son-in-law."

Brooke noticed that SHE wasn't included in Gloria's little zinger about taking care of "her grandchildren and son-in-law," but she let it go.

There was more. Like any woman who moves into the home that her husband once shared with his late wife, Brooke felt the need to make changes so that the house would feel more like her own. She replaced everything: the bed, the color of the paint on the walls, furniture, window treatments, and even the flooring. The house was arranged differently so that it did not resemble the same one that Rachel lived in. True to form,

Gloria asked Brooke, right in front of the children, why she was trying to erase all traces of their mother. She wasn't doing that. She wanted the house to reflect her OWN style, taste, and decor. She wanted it to feel like home. It had nothing to do with wiping away all traces of Rachel.

Gloria's "wedding gift" to Matt and Brooke was a large photo frame containing a collage of family photos of Matt, Rachel, and the children. Gloria never let Brooke forget that this was her daughter's house, and she was relentless in her efforts to keep Rachel's memory alive and well.

Brooke was a sweet woman with the patience of a saint, but it was quickly wearing thin. Gloria still dropped by unannounced, letting herself in with her key. Brooke felt that this was inappropriate and invasive, but she didn't feel that it was her place to address the problem, so when she urged Matt to put a stop to it, he was hesitant, explaining that he didn't want to hurt Gloria's feelings or come off as an ingrate after all that Gloria had done to help him after Rachel died.

Things continued to worsen. Gloria was so bold that she actually rearranged the kitchen cabinets back to the way Rachel had organized them. She brought large photos of Rachel over for the children, telling them to "ask Daddy to put them up on the wall." She would bring meals over, offering to give Brooke some of Rachel's recipes because Matt really missed her delicious cooking. That wasn't all. Gloria would often "compliment" Brooke's appearance, telling her how "natural" or "comfortable" she looked, unlike her Rachel who always took the extra time to "look her best."

At every turn, Gloria undermined Brooke, making her feel inferior, inadequate, and incompetent. She wasn't outwardly critical; she did things in a roundabout way to let Brooke know that she was a poor second to Rachel.

Brooke suggested that they sell the house and buy another one, but Matt refused, insisting that he didn't want to uproot the kids. They had already had enough changes in their young lives, and besides, they were in a great school district and he didn't want to take them away from their friends. Gloria insisted on keeping the same holiday traditions, which were always celebrated at her house. This meant that Matt and Rachel's family were always together, leaving Brooke's family out in the cold. Except for Rachel's absence, mostly everything stayed the same. Something needed to change. Brooke was at her wits' end.

I advised her to tell Matt that new traditions needed to be created and that Matt needed to make it clear to Gloria that he would be developing traditions that would include his new in-laws, namely Brooke's parents. That would send Gloria a clear message that she was no longer the primary "in-law" — the children were her only relatives in this family. Brooke was Matt's wife, after all. As long as Gloria was allowed to rule the roost with her iron fist, nothing was going to change.

"What you permit, you promote," I told her.

The problem was that Brooke was too nice, and most of the time she suffered in silence. She truly loved her stepchildren and wanted them to feel happy and secure, but she was losing her identity in the process.

I suggested that Brooke host holiday dinners, inviting Gloria and her other family members to join them. Also, the locks to the house needed to be changed to stop Gloria from walking in unannounced. Naturally, Matt wasn't comfortable with this, but Brooke could not allow Gloria's tactics to put a wedge between them. I told her to take charge and get a locksmith in there, and after Gloria got wind of it, to simply tell her that it was for "security reasons," explaining that she was always welcome to come over but to call first to make sure that someone was home to let her in.

As for holidays and other celebrations, my advice was for Brooke to explain to Matt that it hurt HER family to be left out and that she would be spending her holidays with them if he insisted on hanging on to Rachel's traditions with his former in-laws. I advised Brooke to encourage her OWN mother to stop by more regularly and to establish her place as Matt's mother-in-law. I also suggested that she invite other couples over every once in a while to get people accustomed to coming over so that Gloria would feel less of a sense of proprietorship around the house. The point was for Brooke to establish her rightful place as the woman of the house, firmly but kindly.

I also thought it would be a good idea to take the kids on a family vacation, perhaps to Disney World, Kings Dominion, or someplace like that. Bobby and Kristin needed to develop happy memories with Brooke and regard her as a mother figure; otherwise, Grandma would continue running the show. Matt wasn't blind to the problem, but he was a nice guy who didn't want to rock the boat or hurt anyone's feelings. The trouble was that no matter what he did or did not do, it was going to rattle somebody's cage.

Things have improved since then. Brooke put some of my suggestions into action but not as much as I would have liked. It's still a battle to keep a lid on Gloria's control freak tactics; Matt hasn't done too much to put his foot down, but Brooke got a little more aggressive with the situation. The locks to the house have been changed, Rachel's photos were packed away, and Brooke rearranged her kitchen cabinets back to the way SHE liked them. She's actually pregnant as I write this, so a lot of the focus is on the excitement of the new baby. Time and circumstances are helping with the transition. Brooke senses a bit of a crack in Gloria's tough exterior, exposing a bit of vulnerability that is understandable. She lost her daughter and she's afraid of her grandchildren drifting away as they get more caught up in their lives with Matt, Brooke, and their future new baby sister. Gloria needs to realize that she is going to lose anything she holds too tightly.

23. TRACES OF LOVE FROM LONG AGO

This chapter is a touchy one. Have you ever come across traces of your widower's sex life with his late wife? Many women have, and it's not a pretty situation.

When Greta married Tom and moved into the house he had shared with Jackie, his late wife, it was messy. Being a bit of a packrat, Jackie wasn't the best housekeeper and Tom never got around to getting rid of her things, so the place looked as if Jackie still lived there. Greta wasn't about to put up with that, especially since there was absolutely no room for HER belongings, so she told Tom that she would be going through Jackie's dresser and closet and packing all her things away. Greta was a neat freak and Tom wasn't the most organized guy in the world, so he was happy to let her whip the place into shape. And what a rat's nest that house was!

Greta sorted through tons of clothing, shoes, handbags, cosmetics, body lotions, shoe boxes full of old photos, matchbooks, memorabilia from weddings, baby and bridal showers, and other events that took place years ago. Some things were set aside to be donated and others were taken out to the trash. When she opened up Jackie's bottom dresser drawer, she got an eyeful of things that she never wanted to see. Apparently, that was where Jackie kept her toys. Greta found a vibrator, dildo, handcuffs, blindfold, lubricants, lingerie, and nude photos of Jackie. Against her better judgment, she mentioned her discoveries to Tom. He sheepishly smiled and admitted that he and his late wife had had a very active and somewhat kinky sex life. Apparently, Jackie was the more adventuresome one of the two, although Tom seemed to be a very willing participant. It turned Greta's stomach. This was a vision that would always stay in her mind.

Gina shared a similar story. Her boyfriend Rich was a widower whose wife Lizzie died when her car was hit head-on by a drunk driver. Rich had dated different women before meeting Gina. They didn't live together but Gina often stayed overnight at Rich's house. One morning after they woke up, she noticed something on the blanket, a spot that looked a little like dried glue or something, so she asked Rich about it. "What is this? Did you spill something on the blanket?"

"No, that's a sex stain." Rich laughed.

"It's WHAT? Eww, GROSS! Why didn't you wash this after you and your last girlfriend left your mark?"

Rich laughed again. "That's not from my last girlfriend. It was from my wife and me."

Gina wanted to vomit. "And you used it over and over with other women without washing it and now with ME?"

Rich didn't bat an eye. "It's not poison, Gina; they're just natural body fluids."

Oh my God. And by the way, Rich wasn't married anymore. A dead woman is NOT "his wife." He needed to refer to her by name, or as his LATE wife.

There were many other similar stories shared with me. One woman found videos of her widower having sex with his late wife. Others found nude or topless photos of late wives. Another woman found a collection of XXX-rated movies that her now-husband had watched with his late wife.

The absolute worst scenario I ever heard came from a woman who recently married the widower she had been seeing. This new wife had a visitor one day, a flashy, attractive woman who stopped by, unannounced, to "introduce" herself to the new wife. In spite of the unexpected visit, the wife was hospitable, welcomed her uninvited guest in and made them some coffee. As the two of them talked, the REAL purpose for the visit came out. The visiting woman and her husband were "friends" with the husband and his late wife; she wanted to build a similar "friendship" with the new wife. It turned out that these "friends" were bisexual swingers who had swapped partners and engaged in group sex with the widower, his former wife, and other couples. Upon hearing about this, the new wife nearly threw up. She quickly informed her visitor that she was not into that type of activity and cut the visit short. After the visitor left, the wife went to pieces and cried until she was gasping for breath. She had absolutely no knowledge about this part of her new husband's past. When she confronted him about it, he was very cavalier. He reacted with amusement, telling his wife that she needed to "loosen up," "let her hair down," "learn to relax and enjoy herself," and "stop being so uptight and narrow-minded." As a result, she never felt the same about her husband again and it ended up destroying the marriage.

What is it with these guys? Men are much simpler creatures. Maybe they see things like this differently than women do. They really don't think it's any big deal. In their minds, the past is the past; what happened before has nothing to do with the here and now. A woman, however, is different. It's not that easy for her to shake it off and let it go. It weighs heavily upon her mind and heart, causing all kinds of fears, doubts, and insecurities to plague her. It consumes her thoughts all of her waking hours.

The women who came across these sexual souvenirs were troubled by their discoveries. They envisioned their widowers having sex with their late wives, wondering if they were being compared to them unfavorably, not just with the sex act itself; they also wondered if their bodies were less attractive and desirable. They feared that their sex lives left a lot to be desired in the minds of their widowers. It was downright demoralizing and emotionally crippling.

As a rule in ANY intimate relationship, it's never a good idea to divulge every single detail about your past. Many things are better left unsaid, but in situations where there's even the slightest chance that something could come back to haunt you, I think full disclosure is necessary at the point when the relationship begins to take a serious turn. It's better for a woman to have all the facts about the man she loves so that she can make an informed decision regarding a lifetime or long-term commitment. There is also the risk of unknowingly being exposed to an STD. It is downright devastating when something like this comes to light after a woman marries her widower or gets into an exclusive, established relationship with him, and then finds out, after the fact, about unsavory or unacceptable sexual behaviors he engaged in.

24. TRANSFORMING YOU INTO HER

Have you ever seen the movie *A Face to Die For*? It's about a young girl who was in a horrible accident that left her face terribly scarred and disfigured. She grew up into a timid, self-conscious woman who had extremely low self-esteem because of her damaged face. Her condition came to the attention of a wealthy and successful plastic surgeon who was confident that he could repair the damage to this young woman's face. The young woman had to undergo a series of surgeries over a period of a year, but in the end, she turned out to be breathtakingly gorgeous — so much so, that the doctor broke his strictest rule and fell in love with his now beautiful patient. On the evening that they announced their engagement at a party in his home, the plastic surgeon's spiteful ex-girlfriend, who was one of the guests, took his now-fiancée aside and led her to a private room in the surgeon's house to show her a portrait of his late wife who was the spitting image of his new fiancée! Yes, that's right…the plastic surgeon had reconstructed the young woman's face to turn it into an identical replica of his first wife who had passed away.

When it comes to women, widowers, like many men, prefer a certain "type." It could be a physical type, a personality type, or whatever. The point is that every guy has his own preferences as to what he desires in a woman.

Jack was a widower married to a tall, slender blonde. Annette was beautiful — a real head turner. About a year or so after she passed away, he started seeing Flossie, a woman who looked so much like Annette that they could have passed for sisters; however, that's where their similarities ended. The two women had completely opposite personalities.

Annette was very much a "go-getter"…gregarious, ambitious, active, and outspoken. She was always pursuing better things, such as a nicer car, fancy clothes, more money, and an overall higher standard of living. Jack admired, respected, and adored her. He was proud of her determined "can-do" nature, and although he was successful in his own right, he was the less aggressive of the two and was happy to follow in Annette's shadow. When she died, the light went out of his soul and his spirit was broken. When he met Flossie, at first glance he was overjoyed. In his grief, he felt like he was getting another chance to bring the sparkle back into his life that had faded after he lost Annette.

Flossie was nothing like her predecessor. She was friendly, in a quiet, laid-back way. She wasn't afraid of hard work, but she wasn't the fireball that Annette was. Flossie had her own small, quiet circle of close friends. She loved cooking, sewing, and making her home a cozy place to live. Jack was always "encouraging" her to "get out there and live life to the fullest." Flossie felt like she was already doing that. Her idea of a quality life was the enjoyment of simple pleasures. She had no desire to be the social butterfly, dine in fancy restaurants, take luxurious vacations, and fill her closet with the latest fashions. She wasn't interested in all the glitz and glamour that Annette loved to pursue. Flossie was a beautiful woman, but her style of dress wasn't flashy like the clothes that Annette wore. Gradually, her self-esteem began to suffer as Jack continued to push her to become more polished and sophisticated.

"Jack makes me feel like I'm never going to be good enough," she told me. "I go out of my way to make him happy, but he's never satisfied!"

In my opinion, Jack had not fully accepted Annette's death and was trying to turn Flossie into the woman he lost. Jack wasn't deliberately being cruel or unkind, but he had no idea how much he was beating Flossie down by trying to chip away at who she was in order to recreate the life he had with Annette. "The problem is with him. There is nothing wrong with you," I told Flossie. "You need to sit down and level with him. You're not Annette. You never WILL be Annette. You have no desire to become Annette. He needs to understand that and accept you for who you are. Don't stick around hoping he'll learn to appreciate you; otherwise, you're only signing up for disappointment and heartache. He's making you feel inadequate, but the truth is that some other guy will consider you to be absolutely perfect. Let go of Jack and hold out for someone who appreciates your uniqueness and special qualities. If you stay with Jack, he will destroy your morale."

Naturally, Flossie didn't want to let go, but by the time she shared her frustration with me, she was at her wits' end. She was beautiful and never had any problem attracting men, but she was a one-man woman, not a player, and she genuinely cared a lot about Jack. Except for his pushing her to be somebody she wasn't, he was a good guy who treated her well and they enjoyed being together. She didn't especially enjoy dating and only wanted to find that one special guy and settle down in a solid relationship.

"Don't settle just to settle down," I advised her.

It took a few months before Flossie gathered the words and the courage to express her feelings to Jack. True to form, she did it kindly and quietly. She ended the relationship on a friendly note and focused on trying to recover from this experience. She dated some and enjoyed a few, short-lived relationships that didn't work out for different reasons, but for the most part she went on with her life.

About a year later, Jack called her out of the blue just to say "hi" and to ask how she was doing. They spoke for a little while and she was happy to hear from him. He had dated a few women but nothing had come of these relationships. All of the women he went out with were Type A personalities like Annette, but they were somewhat jaded and a bit shallow; they lacked quality and substance. Jack found himself missing Flossie's quieter and more solid nature and he wanted to see her again.

"I can't, Jack. My morale took a real beating when I was with you. You want another Annette and I cannot live up to what you're looking for. I don't want to be with someone who can't love me for who I am. No two people are alike and you'll never find an exact replica of Annette, either in looks or personality. You need to bury her, finish grieving, and leave the past behind instead of trying to burden another woman with unreasonable expectations. You don't know how it feels to be in that position; it's a lot of pressure to put on somebody. If you want to call me once in a while to touch base, I'd love to hear from you, but never again will I allow someone to put me in the position of feeling like I'm deficient."

Things went on this way for about another year, with Jack calling Flossie regularly, but she refused to get together with him, even as friends. She didn't trust herself to avoid getting drawn back in again. She continued to date other guys, which upset Jack when he heard about it. The more Flossie refused to budge, the more his desire for her escalated. She had that stubborn determination that he admired so much. It was a part of her that he had never seen before because she was very unobtrusive. He also loved her substance and principles. He became set on winning her back and was willing to do whatever it took to gain her trust and earn a second chance.

His perseverance paid off. Flossie finally agreed to let him take her out to dinner and this time, it was all about HER, not Annette. The differences in him were unmistakable. Flossie's willingness to let him go had ultimately paid off. Her relationship with Jack blossomed as they continued to see each other until he eventually asked for her hand in marriage and she happily accepted.

A grieving widower is not a bad person, but in his sorrow he is not thinking clearly; therefore, if you date a widower, it is YOU who has to have the discernment to recognize whether he's ready to date or if he is merely looking for someone to fill the empty spot in his life.

25. THE MEASURING STICK

Doesn't it just drive you up a wall when your widower's late wife becomes the measuring stick for every event in his life? Let me explain.

Eva was telling me about her relationship with Vince, a man she had been seeing for two years. She noticed that he had a very disturbing habit that started to drive her absolutely crazy. Whenever she and Vince would talk about something, his timeline was always about Sally, his late wife who had died from leukemia. Eva and Vince were talking about going on vacation when she asked him if he had ever been to Niagara Falls.

"I love it there," he replied. "We were there before; it must have been somewhere around 2012 because it was before Sally got sick."

Eva was pissed. "WE were never there before, Vince. YOU were there before!"

"I meant Sally and me," he said.

"I KNOW what you meant, but you and Sally are no longer a 'we' and it makes me feel like a third wheel when you say 'we' when referring to you and Sally." Naturally, this developed into a nasty argument.

Eva tore into Vince. "Every time we talk about anything, Sally always has to come into the conversation! For example, when you told me about that car accident you had, you couldn't think of when it happened until you remembered that it was the day after Sally was first diagnosed with leukemia. And what about the time when your kids took you to that fancy steakhouse for Father's Day? You remembered what year it was because Sally was too sick to go along. Then there was the time that terrible storm knocked your electricity out for two days, and once again, you recall when it happened because it was right after Sally died. The time frame of every single event in your life always revolves around something that has to do with Sally. Dammit, Vince, can you not remember ANYTHING without bringing Sally into the mix?"

Vince gave it right back to Eva. "Sally's illness consumed my life for several years. So naturally there are a lot of 'before and after' events that I remember as taking place either during her good, healthy years, the years that she was sick, and then after she died. So shoot me, for God's sake! What the hell am I doing that is so wrong?"

"It's not just about that, Vince. Even when you mention something from way back, you always talk about it as something that happened before you met Sally or after you started dating Sally or before you and Sally got married or when Sally was pregnant and whatever else was going on with Sally whenever you bring up the past. Can't you talk to me about ANYTHING without using her as the measuring stick to gauge the timeline? How would YOU like it if every time I talked about something, I mentioned that I was married to John or seeing Mike or some other Tom, Dick, or Harry I was involved with at that time? Whether you want to admit it or not, it would get on your nerves, too!"

Vince started to see her point. "I'm not doing it on purpose, Eva. I think you're taking it too personally."

Eva was on a roll. "Maybe so, Vince, but it's getting old. I wish you'd try to speak of your memories in terms of 'I and me' instead of 'us and we' when referring to something that happened in your life before I came along."

At that point, the conversation fizzled out without an ugly, tear-filled scene. The situation never really got resolved but they stayed together with an unspoken agreement to disagree. Vince toned it down some with the Sally nonsense, but when he slipped up and used her as a timeline measuring stick, Eva either ignored it or changed the subject without any fuss.

"It all boils down to choosing your battles," she told me. "Things will never be perfect but they have gotten better. At least I spoke my mind and got it off my chest and Vince HAS made an effort to tone down the Sally references. We have an otherwise decent relationship so I'm not about to throw it all away over this one thing, but to be honest, if I never hear another word about Sally again, it'll be too soon."

26. YOUR PLACE OR MINE?

In many relationships, some women do not live with or marry their widowers for various reasons. A lot of problems can be avoided when each person has their own home. Larry and Vickie were one such couple.

Larry was a widower raising two children. Vickie, his girlfriend, had three kids of her own who shared custody with her ex-husband. Larry and Vickie both worked full-time jobs and they lived about an hour apart from each other.

Larry's two children were not thrilled about the idea of his dating again. Like many children of widowers, they felt like their mother was being forgotten and replaced. They were not supportive and they did everything in their power to push Vickie into the background while keeping their mother's memory alive and active.

Vickie's children were more sensible, well-balanced, mature, and accepting. They were well aware that parents are people and that relationships end for different reasons. They weren't happy that their parents were divorced, but they were accommodating and didn't cause any trouble.

While Larry and Vickie had a good relationship, they had no plans to move in together, at least while they were raising their children, because doing so would be disruptive to their young lives. A fair compromise would be to find a home about halfway between their two houses, but it would still mean that both sets of kids would be uprooted, taken away from their friends and activities, and there was sure to be resentment and hostility on both sides. As a result, Larry and Vickie took turns spending time at each other's houses. Yet this turned out to be the cause of their problems.

Vickie found that she was the one who was doing most of the traveling, spending far more time at Larry's house than he spent at hers. Her shared custody agreement with Joe, her ex-husband, provided her more free time and flexibility. Joe was a decent person and a good father; since he lived nearby, it wasn't a problem getting the kids to and from school. Vickie and Joe had an amicable divorce; they just couldn't live together, but they had a fantastic co-parenting relationship. Vickie got along well with Joe's new wife, Sylvia, so it was a far better situation than most divorced couples have. When her children were with their father, Vickie would spend time at Larry's house. His kids alternated between ignoring her and being openly rude. They jumped on every chance they could to compare her unfavorably to their late mother and made references to their mother's alleged superiority in their efforts to make Vickie feel inadequate. The late wife's photos were all over the house; many of her personal belongings were still there, as well. If anybody walked into that house, they'd never realize that she was deceased because the kids would throw a fit any time Larry would change or remove anything in the house. Their hostility toward Vickie was blatant and unmistakable. Like many widowers, Larry would overcompensate, allowing his kids to get away with far more than he should have because, after all, they missed their mother and they were still grieving. Naturally, the kids played the guilt card for all it was worth. The obvious solution would be for Larry to go to Vickie's house when her kids were with their father. They had their grandparents nearby to look after them, as well as Larry's siblings, who were always happy to help. Larry's family liked Vickie and were thrilled to see Larry happy again and getting on with his life. The problem was that the kids would kick up a fuss whenever their aunts, uncles, or grandparents took care of them because they knew their father was with Vickie and they had no intention of cooperating or making it easy for him to enjoy spending time with her.

Vickie tried to reason with Larry. "It's not fair for me to be doing all the running back and forth. Why can't we alternate weekends at each other's houses?"

Larry did not agree. "My kids already lost one parent. It's hard enough for them to see me with another woman, let alone my disappearing every other weekend."

"Larry, you're not disappearing on them. They can get in touch with you anytime they want and they're even welcome to come over with you, but they want nothing to do with me. I know that you're trying to be sensitive to their feelings, but have you given any thought to MINE? How do you think it makes ME feel to spend a weekend around two kids who resent the very air that I breathe? They accuse me of 'taking over' and whenever you attempt to get rid of anything that belonged to Robin, they blame me and assume that I'm pushing you to wipe out all traces of your late wife. You do absolutely nothing about their behavior. They play you like a harp with that damn guilt card and you fall for it every time! Would you have allowed anybody to get away with treating Robin that way? How about your mother or any of your sisters? Don't try to tell me that it's 'different' because they lost their mother. They are going to face loss and disappointment throughout their lives, but that's not a license to be rude or to take it out on other people. It's not MY fault that Robin died. You and I didn't even meet until a year after she passed away. Why are they allowed to get away with this, Larry?"

Once again, Larry tried to justify their behavior. "They see you as a threat, Vickie. You're the woman I love. My kids said that you've stolen my heart from their mother and that hurts them."

Vickie got angry. "Of COURSE, your heart is with me and no longer with Robin; you cannot love two people at the same time, but I didn't steal anything. Do you think that I woke up one day and said to myself, 'Hmm, let's see if I can meet a nice widower, make him fall in love with me, and forget all about his late wife.' Don't you think that sounds ridiculous? We met and fell in love. What's wrong with that? If your kids had any common sense, they'd realize that you can only be in a relationship with one woman at a time. Do they actually expect you to stay committed to a marriage that no longer exists? C'mon, Larry, you know I'm right! Up until now, I've been patient, but if this crap continues I'm going to give it right back at them. You have two choices: either you insist that your kids respect me when I'm there or you start coming over to MY house, because I'm not going to put up with it any more. I've had enough!"

This is a bad situation with no easy solution in sight. If Larry takes a stand, he feels like he is adding pain to his children's grief. If he doesn't, Vickie will come back at the kids, making an already stressful situation even worse. If Larry spends more time at Vickie's house, he'll feel like he's abandoning his kids.

When Vickie asked me for advice, I had to think about it for a bit, weighing all the factors before offering my opinion. The overall relationship between Vickie and Larry was a very good one and you don't throw away that kind of relationship over one problem. Furthermore, I don't think it's ever a good idea to let kids have a power position over their parents. On the other hand, while Larry might be able to force them to be respectful, he cannot force them to be happy or accepting, and the tension would still exist even if their behavior improved considerably.

True to my nature, I advised Vickie to make it Larry's problem, not hers. She's the adult and if she gave it right back to the kids, she would, in effect, be letting them control her actions. Her best response would be to greatly minimize her exposure to the kids and to spend a lot less time at Larry's house. When they wanted to be together, they could either go out somewhere or go to HER house. She shouldn't be nasty about it and tell Larry that she doesn't want anything to do with his kids, but rather, explain to him that she doesn't want to "upset" the kids by her presence. If Larry complained that his kids would never get used to her if she stays away, Vickie should tell him that she can't get used to being mistreated while they get used to her, which may never happen. If Larry cannot bear the thought of taking an aggressive position with his kids, he's going to have to take what comes with it, which means less quality time with Vickie. If Vickie continues spending time at Larry's house in spite of the fact that his kids are given free rein to mistreat her, she's letting them know that she'll tolerate almost anything for the sake of the relationship and that will only invite more disrespect. Larry needs to decide if he wants to be Vickie's significant other or a puppet for his kids. The point is for Vickie to stay in the relationship while setting boundaries and keeping her self-respect. If Larry wants more from her than what she's giving him, he knows what he has to do.

Vickie put my suggestions into practice. Larry didn't blame Vickie for setting her boundaries; he actually respected her for standing up for herself and not retaliating against his kids. They were HIS responsibility to deal with and Vickie gave him the dignity of handling this problem as he saw fit without letting it make her a victim of the situation. Larry's way of dealing with it was positive reinforcement. He didn't punish his kids for their negative behavior, but instead he rewarded them when they were polite to Vickie. The problems didn't go away overnight but they gradually got better, especially a couple of years later when his kids started dating and became more caught up in their own relationships. Time is a great healer. Memories fade, pain dissipates and life goes on.

27. HE LOVES ME, HE LOVES ME NOT

Do you ever wonder where you REALLY stand in the heart and mind of the widower you love? That's the million-dollar question that many women ask themselves. Does he wish he was still with his late wife instead of me? If he met us both at the same time, whom would he have chosen? Am I just filling the empty spot in his life? Will he always miss her? Is he really over her and ready to move on? Does he think about her more than he thinks about me? How will I ever know for sure where his loyalties lie? Will it ever just be about us?

Let me tell you about one such woman who struggled with this type of uncertainty. When Lana met Marty, their relationship started out great. It was a passionate, heart-pounding, pulse-racing, whirlwind romance that heated up rather quickly. Marty was everything Lana ever wanted in a man; he was exciting, attentive, and totally smitten with her. The relationship was over the top — they couldn't seem to get enough of each other. Marty's friends and relatives were somewhat surprised by the speed and intensity of the relationship, considering that he had been widowed six months earlier. He and Janet, his late wife, had a good, solid marriage. They were very much in love and totally dedicated to each other. This was the second marriage for both of them; each had grown children, but not with each other. Their children were in their late teens when they got married ten years earlier. Janet died as the result of a fall. She was walking down the front steps of their house when she lost her balance and hit her head on the concrete pavement. She was in a coma for about a month before she slipped away. Marty took it hard, but he kept himself busy at work and stayed out of his house as much as possible to avoid dwelling on Janet's death. He was sitting with his tablet at a local coffee shop one Saturday morning when he noticed Lana, an attractive woman about his age who was at the next table on her laptop. They struck up a conversation and things took off from there. It seemed to be a match made in Heaven.

The first sign of trouble came several months later when Lana called him to say "good morning." Marty wasn't his usual, romantic self, but rather, he was somewhat quiet and in a bit of a funk. Lana was thrown off, as she had never seen this side of him. Her attempts to draw him out only made him irritable. "What have I done wrong?" she asked.

"It's nothing," he replied. "I'm just having a bad day. I'll talk to you tomorrow, okay?"

Lana was awake half the night that evening, worrying and wondering what was wrong. Everything seemed so perfect, so what could have caused him to act so cold and distant all of a sudden? She nearly drove herself crazy thinking about all the possibilities. When he called her later the next day, she invited him to come over for dinner. He was back to his old self but Lana could not shake the feeling that something was bothering him. Finally, he told her that the day before was the first anniversary of Janet's death and that he felt overwhelmed. Eager to smooth things over, Lana assured him that these feelings would fade, urged him to focus on the present and let go of the past. Except for Marty's occasional mood swings, things were great between him and Lana, so much so, in fact, that he asked her to marry him and she happily accepted.

They decided to sell their homes and buy a house together. Lana acted quickly. She went through her house, getting rid of a lot of things that had accumulated over the years that she no longer wanted or needed. Much was donated or tossed out. Except for the barest necessities, everything she wanted to keep was packed up. She had a buyer for her house and settlement was only days away. The plan was for her to move into Marty's house until they found one that they wanted to buy, then Marty's house would go up for sale. Wedding plans were made, the invitations were out, and the big day was only about three weeks away when Marty blindsided Lana. He wanted to end the relationship.

"I think we jumped into the marriage plans too quickly," he said. "I don't think I really thought things through and I don't feel ready for this."

Lana was shocked and heartsick. How could he be so devoted to her and then shut it off in the blink of an eye? Something else must be going on, she told herself. Maybe somebody had made him feel guilty. Perhaps it was just pre-wedding jitters. She couldn't believe that he could make such a drastic change from blazing hot to ice cold without warning or notice.

But it turned out that he could and he did. It was over and nothing Lana said made one bit of difference.

Her life was a mess. She had the humiliating and heart-wrenching burden of telling all the invited guests that the wedding was off and cancelling all the arrangements. On top of that, her house was sold and she had to find another place to live.

She quickly rented an apartment and was just getting settled and trying to pick up the pieces of her life when Marty called her. "I'm sorry about what happened, Lana. I never meant to hurt you. I really do love you. I was confused and I guess I just went into a panic. After losing Janet, I began to wonder if I could go through something like that again if anything were to happen to you. I'm so sorry about everything. Can we start over? Please give me another chance. We'll take it slow this time."

Lana foolishly agreed, though her friends and family told her that she was out of her mind for going back to Marty. In spite of repeated warnings, she let her heart be her guide and started seeing him again. She convinced herself that everybody deserves a second chance. Maybe he realized how much he missed her. She believed that their time apart had given him a chance to get his head together and that things would be different this time. His mood swings continued to kick in every now and then, mostly on significant dates. Lana told herself that he would get over it, though she never knew which version of Marty she was going to see from one day to the next. Some days she wondered if his feelings for her were real, and other times she believed with all her heart that he loved her. This was an emotional roller coaster that took a terrible toll on her. Eventually, Marty left her again and this time it was for good. He met another woman — a strong willed, independent one whom he respected. Her name was Amy and she was nobody's fool. Marty chased her around left and right just to get a date with her. He found her to be exciting and he was willing to go to any lengths to have her.

Lana wanted to kick herself for not listening to her friends. For the second time, Marty made a fool out of her. She felt like a doormat and swore to herself that she would never get involved with another widower again.

My feeling was that Marty was, by nature, an inconsistent person. He had that "all or nothing" mentality; as a result, the relationship alternated between high highs and low lows. There was never any stability or predictability to his behavior and maybe this made him more exciting to Lana. I do not believe that this was a widower related issue. I'm not a shrink, but I do know that decent and normal men just don't act that way, even in the midst of grief. Heartache doesn't change a person's basic personality. Even though somebody is deeply sad, they don't become Dr. Jekyll and Mr. Hyde unless it was a pre-existing pattern in them. Lana blamed Marty's behavior on the fact that he was widowed. I chalk it up to his being a jerk. Nice guys don't do things like that. Not everything can and should be blamed on the late wife's death.

Moral of the story: Don't put up with any behavior from a widower that you wouldn't tolerate from any other guy.

28. GUIDELINES AT A GLANCE

Don't be an emotional caretaker. Many women, by nature, are inherent nurturers. We love to soothe and look after those we love. We are often the more sensitive gender in the human race. We hate to see someone suffering and we rush right in there to make them feel better. There's nothing wrong with that. It only becomes a problem when this side of us dominates our actions in a relationship with a widower. If you are involved with a man who has not fully recovered from the death of his late wife, back away and let him work through his grief; otherwise, you're setting a dangerous pattern for yourself.

If you start out being patient, understanding, and compassionate, you are sending the message that you are there to ease his pain. You are providing him with sympathy and companionship, giving him permission to continue wallowing in his misery without any consequences. As a result, you will set yourself up to become a crutch. He will regard you more as a crying towel than a romantic partner. After a while, you will get frustrated when the relationship does not progress in the direction you were hoping it would. Everything will revolve around his grief and loss. When you start pushing for more, he will get frustrated because you are no longer the calm, understanding, supportive person he has come to know. He will start to feel pressured to give you more than he's ready or able to provide. You will grow angry and bitter that you invested so much time to be there for a guy who does not recognize or appreciate all the sacrifices you made in your effort to comfort him. You expect that he should be ready to move on and reciprocate the love that you have given him.

Guard your heart. One of the most challenging things that you will ever do is to love a widower. You need to tread VERY carefully in these shark-infested waters. Think of a widower as a previously owned vehicle on a used car lot. He might look great, sound great, and feel great to be with, but remember…you haven't yet had a good look at everything going on under the hood. It's easy to miss all the flaws and imperfections until you've "driven" him for a while. Also keep in mind that a widower has an agenda. He may not deliberately be trying to dupe anybody, but the fact is that he's probably still grieving, he's lonely, and he's been forced out of his comfort zone by the death of his late wife. He desperately wants to put his world back together with a life that resembles the one he lost when his late wife died. He's looking for the missing piece to the puzzle in his life.

Like any normal person who gets back into the dating game, it's human nature to put one's best foot forward. The widower is no exception. He's not TELLING you that he's looking to fill the void left behind by his late wife. Maybe he doesn't even realize it himself. If his dating profile photos include his late wife, steer clear. You should also read between the lines as to what he writes on his dating profile; even if he IS only looking to fill the emptiness in his life, he's not about to openly advertise that on a dating site. Imagine this profile description: "Lonely widower who lost the love of my life seeking a placeholder for deceased spouse. Looking for a willing partner to satisfy my physical, emotional, and social needs with no expectations of having first place in my heart. Must be flexible and adaptable, cheerfully supporting any and all memorial events, grief fests, posthumous anniversary tributes, birthday parties, and other torch-bearing activities. Martyr-like patience, support, and understanding are a must. A woman who is willing to take a backseat to resentful kids and former in-laws would be a plus."

How many women would flock to THAT profile? My guess is not many. These guys must think that women find it endearing to see a broken-hearted widower who still loves and stays true to a dead woman. Truthfully, there are women out there who would be attracted to such a man. It could be an ego thing or a challenge for them to see if they are irresistible enough to make him forget about his late wife; or worse, they could perceive him as being a man of exceptional loyalty and tenacity, hoping that he would give them the same level of dedication that his late wife had. Don't ever become attracted to a man's potential. He may never live up to your expectations. You will end up feeling disappointed and resentful that you waited patiently for him to get over her and fall deeply in love with you. Don't invest your time or emotional energy trying to turn the wrong man into the right one. You'll get angry that he does not recognize or appreciate the sacrifices you made, and he'll get angry that you're trying to change him.

From all outward appearances, a widower doesn't look or act like he's all broken up. He can't afford that luxury — yet. Later, when your relationship with him becomes more established, you'll get to see his sadness, tears, and the quiet funk he gets into whenever a significant date comes up or something triggers a memory of the late wife. Why would any woman in her right mind sign up for THAT? So, ladies, guard your hearts. Don't be too quick to fall for him, no matter how nice he may be. Keep your emotions well-hidden until you know that you're safe. Wait until you know for sure that you're getting the best of him before you reciprocate accordingly.

Pay attention to his words. When people speak, they are verbalizing what they're thinking. If you're out at a restaurant with your widower and he mentions how much his late wife liked that place, he associates it with her. If you're away on vacation and he starts telling you about his memories of being there with her, such as where they stayed, what they did, etc., you can be sure that it's reminding him of her. Even if you're just sitting around the house making small talk and he mentions his late wife, what he's telling you is that she's on his mind. The best way to handle this is to listen with polite disinterest and a distracted, indifferent demeanor. Don't contribute to the conversation, and as soon as it's appropriate, shift to talking about something else. What you don't want to do is to show any anger or discourage him from bringing her up; otherwise, you will give him the impression that you feel threatened by her and he'll just stop talking to you about her; however, it won't stop him from thinking about her — he'll just keep quiet about it. You want to know how often she crosses his mind so don't make a stink about it. Eventually, his life with you and the memories you make together will take precedence over the past. Best of all, if he feels free to mention her and he brings her name up less and less, you'll know for sure that his thoughts of her are fading further and further into the back of his mind.

Relationship seniority should not equal relationship priority. Men who have been with one woman for a very long time have a hard time letting go. Don't accept it when he says, "I can't help it. She was a part of my life for X number of years. You can't just expect me to act as if she never existed."

That's a cop-out excuse to keep hanging on to the past. It's understandable that he will have certain thoughts, habits, and daily routines that became imbedded as the result of spending so many years with the late wife; however, he should progressively and systematically continue to extricate himself from certain behaviors and traditions that do not fit his life with you. If he can't do that, he should never have ventured out into the dating world, passing himself off as "available." Availability has many facets. He needs to be mentally, emotionally, and psychologically receptive, as well as physically available. When a widower gets involved with another woman while he continues to carry a torch for the late wife, what he's saying to you in effect is, "I don't want to be alone. I need sex and companionship. I need to replace my lost ticket to "couples status." I also love my late wife and want to hang on to her, so please understand that I need you to fill my physical, emotional, and social needs without having to give you my entire heart because it belongs to my late wife."

This is a great opportunity! What a wonderful deal — a fantastic offer! SIGN ME UP! NOT! A widower is a still a man. His late wife didn't have to settle for only a percentage of him and neither should you. It doesn't matter how long he was with her. He's not with her anymore. He's with you now. His mindset, thoughts, and habits should indicate that you are his priority, even if you'll never have the same amount of time with him that the late wife had. Even if the late wife has "seniority," YOU should be his priority.

Don't change to fit in to his routine. The LAST thing in the world that you want to do is to step into the life that your widower had with his late wife and pick up with him right where she left off. This will only make him regard you as an extension of her and not a person in your own right. Continue doing whatever it was that you were doing before he came along and make him adapt to YOU; otherwise, you could lose the very quality that attracted him to you in the first place. Worst of all, you're teaching him that you can be molded to fit into whatever area of his life has the greatest need. Just do what you would be doing if you hadn't met him. If you always went to the gym on Saturday morning, don't stop, even if it's the only day you both have off. Let him figure out how to fit into YOUR schedule. The harder he has to work to be with you, the more he will value and appreciate the time that you are together. If he wants to be with you strongly enough, he will find a way. Look at the late wife. She's dead and gone; therefore, she can no longer do ANYTHING to get the widower's attention, yet she still remains in his thoughts. If a man loves you, he'll take you any way he can get you. Don't worry that he'll get discouraged and find someone else. A decent guy would rather have limited time with a quality woman he really cares about than all the time in the world with a woman he doesn't like as much.

Most importantly, you don't want to set a dangerous precedent. If you start off being too accommodating, he's going to expect you to fit into HIS world, no matter what it costs you, and that may include parts of the life he shared with his late wife. Start the relationship off right. If he becomes conditioned to your treating your own priorities as if they matter, he will respond accordingly. Put yourself on the back burner in order to show him how nice and easy-going you are and you'll be training him to regard you as secondary. You'd be surprised at how these little things escalate into big ones. One little germ can take down an entire body. Once you "poison" the relationship by acting as if HIS wants, needs, feelings, and schedule matter more than yours, you're setting the stage for disrespect, heartache, and disappointment. So, don't stop doing what you're doing. Do NOT let him mold you into becoming more like his late wife and, most importantly, don't let him get you into the same routine (or rut) he was in with her. He needs to understand that you're NOT her. Her memory should never contaminate your relationship — ever.

Don't grovel for approval. This is another important point. If you're the first woman who came on to the scene after the late wife died, you'll get the brunt of it, as the woman whom the widower broke the ice with. You'll be scrutinized and dissected by the people in his life, many who may be looking for a reason to dislike and discredit you. Secretly, people will compare you to the late wife. You did nothing wrong…unless you happen to be the one who caught the heart of a widower. There will always be those who aren't ready to see him move on. More often than not, it's his children. It doesn't matter whether they're minors or adults. The fact is that they can't bear to see Daddy with any woman who isn't their mother. They would prefer that he remain lonely and stuck in his grief. It hurts them to see him being happy without their mother.

Some people in your widower's life may tolerate you with forced politeness. Others may be openly hostile. The most common reaction for the woman in this position is to go all out to win the approval and acceptance of these people. Do yourself a favor: Don't grovel. The greater the lengths you go to in order to ingratiate yourself to these people, the more they'll despise you. They'll lose all respect for you. Nothing you do will make one bit of difference because they simply don't want to like you.

The best way to avoid rejection is not to seek approval. Don't jump through hoops to win people over. They either want you in their lives or they don't. Avoid being in their company if they make it clear that they don't accept you. You don't want to be around anyone who doesn't want to be around YOU. Be indifferently polite, as you would to a stranger whenever you can't avoid being in their presence. If they want you in their lives, they know where to find you. Remember, you're in a relationship with your widower, not the people in his life. If there's a rift between you and his other loved ones, it's because they created one. My approach is to surround myself with those who like me and appreciate my company. I have no time or interest trying to insinuate myself into the lives of people who have no desire to interact with me. Besides, it's demoralizing to keep exposing yourself to constant rejection. Enjoy your relationship and forget about those people in your widower's life who do not accept you. They're HIS problem to deal with — not yours. Never try to force or push yourself onto anybody who doesn't want you. All you're doing is giving them the satisfaction of snubbing you over and over again. Your presence is a constant reminder that their loved one is gone and they want to punish you for that. Not your circus, not your monkeys.

You may think that your widower's loved ones will dislike you even more for acting as if you don't care about them either way, but the truth is that they ALREADY dislike you just for the fact that you're the woman who stole the heart that once belonged to their dearly departed loved one. Don't kowtow to them. You shouldn't waste your effort trying to atone for a sin that you did not commit. You're guilty as charged simply by the fact that you're in a relationship with the widower. Your efforts should be spent on those who value your presence. You'd be surprised at how this changes the perception of those who don't want you around. They will develop a grudging respect for you if they see that their actions have absolutely no impact on you. Don't ever give anyone a power position over your life. You'll be a happier person for it.

Don't think of yourself as Plan B. One of the biggest complaints I hear from women involved with widowers is that they feel like a consolation prize. He had his life all mapped out and it was cut short with the passing of his late wife. He enjoyed all his "firsts" with her, but that life is gone. Now he's with you. It's no surprise that you feel like the default partner. You suspect that you're second choice and only in his life because she can't be. Before you start thinking of yourself as a cheap imitation, second choice, a back-up partner, a shock absorber, or a consolation prize, consider this: He may have been with the late wife for several years. He started his life with her when he was very young and he hasn't had much dating experience in many years. He got into a very comfortable rut with her, and being a creature of habit, he became set in his ways. Perhaps he thinks she was perfect…they grew and evolved together and acclimated themselves to each other. They had years to work out the bugs in their relationship. She is the one with whom he is familiar, but that doesn't make her particularly special. He just never had anyone else to compare her to. He doesn't know anything different than his life with her. Many women would appear to be perfect if they were the only woman their husbands had ever known intimately.

The truth is that your widower has become a different person since he's been with you. A lot of who he is today has changed in the process of the transition he made from his past life with his late wife to the one he enjoys with you today. He has experienced a new and different lifestyle since he's been with you, and it is those experiences that have changed him from the person he was back then to the person he has become. If the late wife could come back to life, she would find your widower to be a very different man than the husband she once knew. His life has changed, evolved, and expanded since she's been gone; therefore, they might not even be compatible anymore. He would more than likely prefer to stay where he is today with you than return to being the person he was with her, even if he won't admit it. In fact, it may not even be possible for him to regress. A butterfly cannot return to being a caterpillar.

A widower may think that his previous marriage was great only because he never knew anything better. Yet, he might never want to concede that he's happier and better off with you for a few reasons:

1. Respect for the memory of his late wife;
2. He doesn't want to give you the satisfaction;
3. He feels a sense of guilt for being happier with you; and/or
4. He may feel a sense of loyalty to his children or others who loved the late wife.

The bottom line is that you should consider yourself to be an upgrade, not Plan B. Look at it as your widower getting bumped up to first-class when he met you. You will be the one who opens up his world to new and exciting things that he never experienced with his late wife. She did everything she was ever going to do with him. She's history. Her part in his story is over and her time with him is finished.

Remember, she had all of his firsts, but you'll have all of his lasts. It's not who a person starts out with that matters — it's who they end up with. The best is always saved for last. So don't fret because you weren't his first love, because you will be last and BEST love.

<u>Don't badmouth the late wife</u>. This is important, for your own sake. First of all, you'll sound like a she-devil for speaking ill of the dead. Secondly, you'll appear to be threatened or intimidated by her memory. This is especially true if you never met her. You may have heard many negative things about her, but take the high road. By the same token, don't make any positive comments about her either, even if you DID know her. Bringing her up only reminds him of her and keeps her memory alive. If you disagree with things you know about her, such as her habits, her décor, her recipes, or her style of dress, there's nothing wrong with sharing your opinion. Just make sure your comments are legitimate and not mean-spirited. If the situation warrants it, just say what you have to say and then let it go. If you keep harping on him about her, you'll appear to be obsessed and be thought of as feeling inferior to her. In a nutshell, the perception must be that she is the absolute furthest thing from your mind and that his life with her has absolutely no impact on you whatsoever.

That being said, I see nothing wrong with speaking up if he tries to push you into adapting to her habits. You should be loved and appreciated for your own unique qualities. So, yes, speak up if you must, but make it about the SITUATION and not the late wife. Remember, she's not the one doing anything to hurt you.

Most importantly, you should never badmouth the late wife, because you're letting your widower know that she has the power to throw you off balance. It's tantamount to giving him a blueprint of your most sensitive areas. He'll learn exactly which buttons to push if he wants to keep you emotionally off balance and jumping through hoops for his approval. If he knows that he can keep you feeling inferior and insecure, he may use that to his advantage. You should never make an issue out of anybody or anything that means less than nothing to you. People often feel compelled to criticize someone who intimidates them so that they can feel better about themselves by comparison. Don't try to blow out her candle to make yours look brighter. It'll only backfire. You don't like her. You don't dislike her. You feel nothing. You're absolutely indifferent and apathetic toward her. She's the furthest thing from your mind. If he mentions her, listen with polite disinterest with no reaction or comment, then continue doing whatever you were doing. No reaction = no attention = no reward.

Be very happy if you're different than the late wife. I cannot even begin to tell you how many women have lamented the fact that they're so different than their widower's previous wife.

People tend to gravitate toward that which is comfortable and familiar, but if that isn't the case, there's a reason. Women involved with widowed men tend to romanticize his previous marriage and torture themselves with the belief that theirs was a fairy tale. People are always remembered as being far better in death than they actually were in life. Their good qualities are exaggerated, their faults forgotten, and bad characteristics minimized. This is the norm whenever anybody dies, and it's especially difficult when you're coming into a widower's life only to hear glowing comments from others about how wonderful or perfect his late wife was.

I'm going to use automobiles as an analogy. Think about a young guy who recently becomes old enough to drive and he gets his very first car. A few years later, his first car is no longer functional and cannot be repaired, so it ends up in the junkyard — a grave for dead automobiles. In the young man's mind, that car will always have sentimental value for him because it was the first one he ever owned. He'll forget about all the times it broke down, didn't start, and some of the problems he had with it. In any event, the car is gone, he has to get another one and he wants his next car to be a different make and model than what he had. At this point, the guy is older, more mature, a better, more experienced driver, and his financial situation has greatly improved. Think of yourself as his chosen, new, high quality, late model car. You're getting a better, more experienced driver. Most of his accidents and fender benders took place in his first car. He's a much more established and responsible driver with his new vehicle and he's far more inclined to appreciate it and take better care of it than the first car he owned when he was an inexperienced driver.

Even if you believe that the late wife was superior to you because she was more attractive, successful, a better cook and housekeeper, had a nicer figure, and a more exciting, charismatic personality or whatever, don't let that bother you. Not all quality can be measured by physical beauty, talent, or financial success. He might be far more interested in what's under the hood. Don't ever underestimate the value that your widower places on you. There's a reason why he wants a different make and model this time around. If you're the exact opposite of his late wife, chances are that he appreciates qualities in you that he did not find in her.

The fact is that most people improve with age. You're getting the finest, most superior version of him as the result of what he learned from all the youthful mistakes he made the first time around. Furthermore, people often make different choices when they get older. Perhaps your widower would never have married his late wife had he met her later in life. The woman who caught his attention during his youth may not interest the man he is today. Whatever the reasons, he chose you even though you may be the exact opposite of his late wife. Take it as a compliment.

There's a difference between a jerk and a widower. Don't confuse the two. If he's thoughtless, inconsiderate, and insensitive, don't make the mistake of chalking his actions up to grief. A genuinely nice guy isn't cruel and uncaring when he's hurting. Not all behaviors have to do with his widowed status. Chances are that he was a louse most of his life. Many women are overly patient, understanding, and compassionate due to the assumption that the widower they love is still trying to work through his loss. That's a load of crap. For one thing, if he still needs to process his grief, he's not ready for a relationship. I repeat: Do not tolerate anything from a widower that you would not put up with from any other man.

Don't romanticize his previous marriage. No matter what he told you or what you heard others say, NO marriage is a match made in Heaven. Even the best ones have their ups and downs. Your widower and his late wife argued, got on each other's nerves, and fought during their marriage; they struggled with bills, disappointments, daily irritations, and other disruptions in their lives. Toilets overflowed, washing machines broke down, dinners got ruined, etc. Theirs was a marriage with the usual problems...never believe otherwise. You rarely hear about the battles and hardships a widower had during the course of his marriage with his late wife. Instead, it seems as if their lives were like a fairy tale. They weren't.

If he did it to you, he did it to her. One common misconception that many women have is that their widower doesn't treat her half as well as he did his late wife. If he is sarcastic, impatient, and demanding with you, he was the same way with her.

Don't make the mistake of believing that he treated her like a princess up until the day she died, then turned into a jerk after he got involved with you. Whatever bad behavior he shows with you, he showed with her, too. Perhaps she handled it differently. After many years together, they developed their own manner of dealing with their differences. The personality of that marriage was different than it is in the widower's relationship with you. He will quickly learn that his behavior with you will have a very different outcome than what he came to expect from his late wife. Never assume that he was a better man with her. Whatever you are getting from him is the same as what his late wife had. You're not her; therefore, the only difference is in the way you respond to and deal with his actions.

<u>Don't participate in any memorializing activity in the late wife's memory</u>. Let's face it, there are a lot of very valuable fundraising organizations whose profits go toward the research for a cure or supporting people and the families of people who are afflicted with some kind of illness or condition. I would never suggest that you refuse to support a worthy cause; after all, it may someday benefit you or someone you love. If you believe in it, promote the cause but not its affiliation to the memory of the late wife. Make sure that whatever cause you participate in or support, never let it be about her. You don't want to bring any attention to or focus on the late wife. No audience, no show.

<u>If a widower still has too much "late wife baggage," he needs to unpack</u>. One of the biggest red flags is that he keeps his relationship with you a secret. Set and stick to your boundaries. Never tell him what to do or when to do it, but DO let him know that it feels awkward to be hidden away like some shameful habit. A widower who cares about you and loves being with you will want to shout it out to the world and introduce you to the closest people in his life. Don't include him in every part of your life unless he does the same for you.

Even if your relationship is out in the open, you need to speak up if certain things make you uncomfortable. For example, if he is still wearing his wedding ring, it's an indication that he's still committed to his late wife. Perhaps his finger feels bare without it or he promised his late wife he'd never take it off. No matter what his reasons are, it's disrespectful when a widower is involved with a woman while wearing the ring that signifies his commitment to his late wife. Said one woman to her widowed lover, "How do you think your late wife would feel if she knew how you touched me with the hand that wears that ring?" That question hit him like a ton of bricks and off came the ring.

If his wedding photo or pictures of the late wife are in full view or her ashes are prominently displayed in a highly visible area of his house, don't demand that he remove them — it's HIS house, after all, and he has every right to do whatever he wants. By the same token, you have choices, too. Let him know that it makes you uncomfortable and that you won't be spending any time at his house as long as these visual reminders of his late wife are in your face. Tell him that you will either go out with him or spend time with him at YOUR place. If he truly cares for you, he will do whatever it takes to make you feel welcome and comfortable in his home. Your happiness should be his highest priority. Remember that the late wife didn't have to live with the spirit of another woman and neither should you. His life should revolve around his relationship with you in the here and now. You should NEVER be a part of any three heart relationship. He needs to understand that he cannot be one hundred percent all in with you if a part of him is still stuck in the past with his late wife. A divided heart belongs to no one.

Become what you want to attract. Nothing is more appealing than a woman who is genuinely upbeat, confident, and happy with herself. You don't need to make demands on your widower for him to move Heaven and Earth to make you happy. How is it done? You do it by using positive reinforcement. You should never nag, beg, or make demands. All that does is let him know that his actions have a huge influence over your quality of life. We teach people how to treat us by our actions. When your widower does something that pleases you, reward him with your time, attention, and affection. Whenever there is too much mention or focus on his late wife, withdraw and make yourself scarce until he is ready to put you first, above everyone and everything else. You're a gift, not a given. Remove yourself from any situation that is undeserving of your valuable presence.

Someone suggested that these methods are a form of passive aggression or manipulation. I beg to differ. We all know what happens when we give men ultimatums or make empty threats without following through. We are perceived to be demanding control freaks and we lose credibility. Negativity begets negativity. We reap what we sow. All it takes is a considerable level of confidence and self-respect. You don't need to be particularly beautiful or stand out in any special way to be attractive. You simply refuse to engage in anything that does not suit you or meet your standards. Even if you don't feel all that sure of yourself, act as if you do. You should never verbally insist on having your own way. Don't argue or force any demands down your widower's throat. Calmly let him know how you feel, then drop it and watch what he does about it. Don't act hurt, show vulnerability, or play the part of the victim.

If he wants to spend time with you, he has to become somebody who deserves your company. It's that simple. This includes his children and other people in his life. If they ignore you or treat you badly, don't respond with tears and complaints about how hurtful they are. Just go about your business happily and stay away from situations where you're made to feel unwanted or unwelcome. It's very empowering to be emotionally independent. The most effective person is one who has no need or desire for anybody's acceptance or approval. Once your widower realizes that you cannot be easily rattled, it'll shake HIS confidence and weaken any stronghold he has over you. If your widower truly cares about you, he will put you on a pedestal and he won't tolerate anyone treating you with disrespect, especially if it means that he has to face the risk of losing you.

Let your actions speak for you, stand your ground, and don't back down. It won't take him long to realize what he has to do to earn an important place in your life. If he doesn't make the necessary changes to keep you happy and close to him, then you have a decision to make. You have only two choices: (1) Stay in the relationship and accept everything that comes with it, or (2) Remove yourself from any situation where you're not prioritized and respected. Your widower's response will tell you everything you need to know. This approach works in ALL relationships — not just those involving widowers.

<u>Not everything is about you or the late wife</u>. If your widower is in an unpleasant mood, don't press him for an explanation about what might be bothering him. Many women beat themselves up, worrying about the possibility that their widower was thinking about his late wife and fell into a depression. He may be moody by nature. Perhaps he had a bad day at work. Maybe something else is troubling him. There could be a million reasons why he's not at his best. If the two of you have been getting along well without any recent arguments, you shouldn't assume that you inadvertently did something to cause him to withdraw or become irritable. If he's in a funk, don't jump in there to try to fix him. Men do better when they're left alone to sort through their feelings and work things out in their own minds, free of any pressure. Not everything is your fault. Most importantly, don't assume that everything that affects him has something to do with his late wife. If something appears to be bugging him, don't push him for an explanation and don't offer to help him with it. If he wants to talk to you about it, he will. If not, simply detach, go run an errand, or get busy taking care of a neglected chore around the house. Do whatever you have to do, but stay off his back and out of his way. He will love and respect you far more if you don't appear to feel responsible for every facet of his life.

<u>Keep the focus on yourself</u>. At the risk of being repetitive, I cannot emphasize this enough. Remember, he is a man first and a widower second. By the very act of getting involved with you, he is, in effect, sending the message that he has fully recovered from the loss of his late wife and is ready to move on and should be treated accordingly. Don't "handle with care" as if he is some delicate flower that will wilt under a little heat. He must be held to the same rules and standards as any other guy. Don't put yourself on the back burner to coddle him. Don't push your own needs and feelings aside to prioritize his. This will only condition him to view you as less significant than himself. He will appreciate and respect you more for sticking to your principles and staying true to yourself.

<u>Let your actions speak for you</u>. As I mentioned previously, we teach

people how to treat us by the way we treat ourselves. A widower doesn't corner the market on grief and loss. He's not the first person in the world to lose a spouse or loved one, and he won't be the last. Don't stop living your life to give him special care and attention. Even if he has young kids who are going through a rough time, don't assume that it's your responsibility to jump in there and fix everybody, even if you're married or living with him. If he wants your help, he'll let you know. If the kids are rude and hostile toward you, back away. By doing so, your actions are sending the message that disrespect will not be tolerated and that your feelings merit equal consideration. If they lash out at you, go out for a while and let them fend for themselves. Do some shopping, have some coffee with a friend, or just take a ride to shake it off and cool down. Losing a parent or a spouse does not give them a free pass to treat you like a non-entity. You are just as important as everybody else and they need to understand that. If they do not appreciate your presence, give them the gift of your absence. Pain is no excuse for bad behavior. Once your widower or his children realize that you're not about to let them use their grief as an excuse to mistreat you, they will respect and prioritize you. Love and respect go hand in hand.

<u>The terms and conditions of the relationship are not just his to dictate</u>. Another one of the biggest complaints I hear from women who are involved with widowers is that he's "not ready" to make a full commitment. This encompasses a lot of different dynamics. He might not be ready to let go of some of the late wife's belongings or her ashes. Maybe he's not ready to put her photos away or take off his wedding band. It could also be that he's not ready to bring your relationship out in the open. Even if that's not the case, he may not be ready to propose or make your relationship official. Perhaps he's extremely sensitive to what his kids are feeling and is, therefore, not ready to confront them about ignoring you or treating you with disrespect. Perhaps he's still grieving and not yet ready for anything more than sex and companionship, also known as "friends with benefits." This kind of relationship affords him all of the advantages of a relationship with none of the responsibilities. Well, let me tell you, as long as this excuse works for him, he won't have any motivation to do otherwise. As the old expression goes, "Don't buy the cow if you can milk it for free." Are you afraid that you'll lose him if you demand more respect? Does being a doormat give you the love and security you need from this relationship? I think not. As I said, he is a man first and a widower second. He must be held to the same level of accountability as any other man.

If he's ready to have all of HIS needs met, yet not ready to reciprocate, then take a step back. Stop being so predictable and definitely make yourself less available. If he wants to know why you're not around as much, simply remind him that he's "not ready" for the whole enchilada, so you're staying out of his way to give him some "space" to work through his grief. He might insist that he needs you around and that's when you let him know, kindly of course, that YOU'RE "not ready" to take the risk of getting hurt and since he's "not ready" to meet YOUR needs; YOU need to take a step back until he works through his issues. Remember, a partial commitment is a non-commitment.

The point that you need to get across to him is that he cannot have it both ways. If he wants to wear the widower's halo and play the grief card, he's welcome to do so but not at your expense. Funny how quickly these guys recover and become "ready" for more if they realize their tactics don't provide the desired advantages. Are you worried that he'll find a more easygoing, flexible woman to give him everything he wants, expecting nothing in return? Don't be. Women like that are a dime a dozen. You're not one of them. They might get about five minutes of a man's attention, but that's the most they'll get from him and they certainly won't gain his respect. How could they? They don't even respect themselves. No man appreciates a woman who is there for the taking, who hands herself over to him on a silver platter. A widower will tire of this type of woman before he even zips his pants back up. If you can lose a man that easily, you never really had him because his feelings for you aren't strong or genuine. He only wants to get his needs met and you'd eventually end up losing him anyway, along with your self-respect. Don't let your compassion compel you to feel sorry for him or his kids so much that you allow them to cross your boundaries.

Let him play his widowed status for all it's worth if that's what he wants, but he needs to understand what comes with it. He is often regarded as being vulnerable and fragile; as a result, some women will tiptoe around him, handling him with kid gloves. Don't make the mistake of doing the same thing. This means that you should NEVER put your own needs and feelings aside to give him more than you would to any other man; otherwise, you will only reinforce his sense of entitlement. You'd be surprised how quickly he'll recover and become ready to move forward with a woman he cannot manipulate. He will love and respect you if he can't play you. The terms and conditions of the relationship should not be just his to dictate.

Time is your friend. I can't count the number of times I have heard women moan over their fear that they will never "measure up" to the late wife in their widower's heart. Believe me when I say that this is SO not true. It might feel that way at first because you have not developed as much of a history with him as he had with the late wife. Time is your friend. As the years go on, he will create more and more memories with you. His extended family will grow and expand as his children, nieces, and nephews get married to people who have never known the late wife. The same holds true when babies are born into his family. You will be the only woman they will ever associate with your widower. You will experience things with him that his late wife never did. You will be a part of his life experiences that she never was. Keep in mind that a fire goes out for lack of fuel. The void of a person's absence cannot continue to exist when new people and situations factor in and change the dynamics. Whatever habits and traditions your widower developed with his late wife will fade out as he builds new ones with you. The longer she's gone, the more her essence will fade into obscurity. In the meantime, it feels like an agonizingly slow process. Time is your friend. Seconds turn into minutes. Minutes turn into hours. Hours turn into days. Days turn into weeks. Weeks turn into months. Months turn into years. Years turn into decades. Every single moment that the late wife is out of the picture will push more and more of her out of the equation. Don't dwell on her. Focus on enjoying your relationship and making it as fun and enjoyable as possible. As long as your widower is happy with you in the present, he'll have no need or desire to stroll down Memory Lane, but if he does happen to go back there from time to time, don't go along for the ride. It'll be a very lonely and unfulfilling trip with nothing but dim memories that no longer sustain him. Let time work its magic.

If he doesn't make the appropriate adjustments for you, he's not ready. Widowers who have worked through their grief, accepted their new normal and have adapted to the loss of their late wives don't need to struggle to adapt. The late wife may be invisible, but it does not mean her presence is no longer felt, especially if your widower engages in posting sentimental stuff on social media, or letting others treat you "less than" because of circumstances not relevant to your current relationship. Remove the widower label, and you still have a man who needs to behave respectfully in his current relationship, and not for the memories of any former relationships.

Naturally, as in any new relationship, there is always a period of adjustment as you get to know one another and build a foundation that works well for both of you. No two relationship personalities are the same. There are completely different dynamics with you than what he had with his late wife. You, too, will interact with him differently than what you did with the men in your past. There is always a transitional period when a relationship is in the process of becoming established. This is normal in ANY relationship, whether one is widowed, divorced, or never married. The problems arise when your widower has trouble adjusting due to issues related to the late wife. Maybe he feels guilty, as if he's being unfaithful. Perhaps he's afraid of how his children or former in-laws will react to his moving on. Whatever the obstacles are, if he's unwilling to set aside any kind of attachment to the late wife in order to move full speed ahead with you, he's just not ready. Her photo should not be on his computer or phone screen. He should not be carrying pictures of her in his wallet or speaking of her in the present tense. He should not be wearing his wedding band. Her name should not come up regularly. It's normal to mention any former lover or spouse from time to time, but when these memories have the power to keep a widower from moving on, he's not ready. As I said in an earlier part of this book, the only thing he may really be ready for is to escape the pain, emptiness, and void of his loss. I don't believe that a widower deliberately sets out to dupe a woman or to use her to ease his pain, so YOU have to be the one with discernment. Don't assume that it's true when he tells you that he's ready to move on. He may genuinely believe what he's saying, but his actions are the real indicator of what's in his head and heart. Watch what he does and how he deals with the transition and then you can decide whether or not you want to accept what he has to offer. Bottom line: before giving your heart to a widower, make sure that he's looking for love, not help.

Don't blame your widower for the actions of others. As I mentioned earlier, a widower may be ready to move on, but he could hesitate because those closest to him are not ready to see him do so. They may tolerate you with forced politeness or treat you with outright contempt. What they do isn't his fault and he cannot make them accept you, but he SHOULD insist that they respect you. If he allows others to get away with mistreating or ignoring you, it means that he's more concerned about their feelings than yours. This doesn't mean that he should hang all over you with mushy displays of affection, but he shouldn't be afraid to let everybody know how much he cares about you. At some point, they have to own their grief without trying to forcefully transfer it over to him. We have no control over the amount of time other people spend grieving, the actions of his children, the late wife's family, or anything else that involves the death of his late wife, for that matter. If he's afraid to be open about his feelings for you, there's nothing you can do except to minimize your exposure to negative or ill-mannered people. Don't argue about it or try to force yourself on anybody who doesn't want you. Simply hold your head up with an air of dignity, don't take any nonsense and remove yourself from the equation. Remember: Insecurities are loud. Confidence is quiet.

Choose your battles wisely. Whenever people get involved with each other, there are sure to be some pieces of their past that show up from time to time. This happens whether they are divorced or widowed. Don't make a thing out of it every time you see a reminder of the late wife, whether it be an item of hers that was somehow not disposed of or some other reminder that she was there before you. We have all had a history before we met our current partners. Don't nitpick. As long as the relationship is an otherwise good one and the focus is on the present and not the past, leave it alone.

It's also not a good idea to confront him on the late wife's birthday, their former wedding anniversary, or her date of death to ask him if he's okay or whether he's thinking of her. She may have crossed his mind, but it's also possible that she didn't. Just don't mention it to him; all you'd be doing is bringing these dates to the forefront of his mind and giving him the impression that you're obsessed with her. Leave well enough alone.

Don't feed into ridiculous remarks. One widower actually told his fiancée that she should "appreciate and honor" his late wife because she made him the man he is today. That, my friends, is a load of bull. In every experience and relationship you have ever had, you learned valuable life lessons. Does that mean that every man you were ever involved with should be "appreciated and honored" because they helped to mold you into the person you are today? What about a teacher who made a significant impression on you? How about your parents, grandparents, and siblings or all the people you were friends with, went to school with, or worked with over the years? Think about it. We can all argue that past relationships made you who you are today. How about old flames? You might not feel anything for them now, but you loved them once. How about the father of your children? Without them, you wouldn't have kids and you wouldn't be the person you are today. Didn't THOSE relationships contribute to who you are today, and if that's the case, shouldn't they ALL be appreciated and honored? You can go on and on. You would never be able to keep track of everybody who made some kind of impact on your life. Meanwhile, the woman who is the widower's partner in the present is made to feel insignificant or at least really uncomfortable at the suggestion that she should "appreciate and honor" his late wife. Life is a series of changes and experiences. We are a culmination of EVERYTHING we have lived through and ALL the people who have crossed our paths. If a widower insists on giving all the credit for who he is today to his late wife, it's just a diversionary tactic to try to manipulate you into second-guessing your feelings and questioning your beliefs. Don't feed into this garbage.

A Final Word

I hope that everything I wrote has touched as many of you as possible. I did my best to address the most common challenges that come into play when getting involved with a widower. My comments are a culmination of what I have discovered in my research with women in this position. Your social status, ethnic background, economic situation, or geographical location makes no difference whatsoever. The one common denominator we all share is that the man we love is a widower and, like any other relationship, it has its own set of challenges and requires a certain period of adjustment. Only you and you alone know how much you're capable of handling. There are no right or wrong answers and no "one size fits all" solutions. Whatever works for you is what is right for you. Whatever you read here is strictly my opinion or the opinions of those who have shared their stories with me. Feel free to take what you like and disregard the rest. The most important thing is that we are all bonded by our love for a widower and the desire to be happy. Trust your gut and let your intuition be your guide. Finally, be happy and be true to yourself, and the man you love will follow your lead.

29. A WORD TO THE WISE WIDOWER

This section is designed to speak directly to the widower. Perhaps you're too close to the situation and too emotionally charged to get through to him. Maybe if he sees this chapter, it will give him a better understanding of what it's like to be in your shoes.

Dear Widower,

If you're reading this, you're very fortunate to have a woman in your life who loves you very much — enough that she gave you this chapter to read.

The very fact that you got involved in this relationship sends the message that you have recovered from the loss of your late wife and are ready to move on. This is why the woman in your life gets upset when you hang on to your late wife's belongings, continue to wear your wedding band, carry on her holiday traditions, visit the cemetery, or hang on to her ashes, and keep the memory of your late wife alive in various other ways.

Don't get me wrong. This book is NOT a late wife basher. It is not designed to suggest that you had no right to mourn her passing. It's not unreasonable for you to remember a woman who was a big part of your life for many years. Everybody grieves differently and for different periods of time. The point is that you should never bring a new woman into your life while your late wife is still very much on your mind and in your heart. You're doing the next woman an injustice by passing yourself off as available when you're still very much married in spirit to your late wife.

Take all the time you need to recover from your loss. THEN move on with somebody else. Just don't go looking to get involved with a woman to provide companionship and to meet other needs that your late wife isn't around to satisfy. By doing so, you are using an innocent woman who desires a meaningful relationship with a man who can offer her his all, not just selective portions that your late wife can no longer have.

Keep in mind that the new woman in your life doesn't feel what you feel about your late wife. She means nothing to her. She may have her own dearly departed loved ones to mourn; she doesn't want or need to carry your grief, as well. It's not about being selfish or insensitive, but rather a matter of self-respect and refusing to settle for a man who still has a part of himself attached to another woman. She deserves to have nothing less than what you gave to your late wife. If this isn't something you're capable of, please be honest about it, and feel free to find a woman who is willing to settle for a three heart relationship.

One of the most heartbreaking things a woman may have to experience in life is to fall head over heels in love with a widower and see pictures of his engagement and wedding to someone else on his walls. Do you know how it feels for her to see your memories from another woman's life, knowing that the only reason it is possible for her to be in a relationship with you and your children is because another woman is dead? She does not want to pretend that your late wife never existed. After all, she is the mother of your children and she always will be, but she is not your wife anymore. She is not part of your new relationship. For her, as the new woman in your life, to want your full self as her own is not an unreasonable expectation. She deserves a clean slate with you just like any other woman deserves in a relationship. Just because your late wife is no longer walking this Earth does not mean that her footprint isn't still here.

When you refer to a deceased spouse as your "wife" and her family as your "in-laws," you're speaking of your past life in the present tense, creating the perception that your mind and heart are still attached to that part of your life. What you're saying, in effect, is that you're still a married man. If that's how you feel, then you're a cheating husband. Widowers have LATE wives, period. Unless you want to be perceived as a two-timer or polygamist, you should only be with one woman at a time. Your CURRENT spouse or significant other is your one and ONLY partner, period. There are no sister wives. You and she and the late wife do NOT make three.

Don't get angry at the woman in your life for her alleged "insensitivity" when she shows no compassion for your loss. The fact is that if you have not yet completely let go of the past, you should wait before getting involved in another relationship. It's a selfish decision on your part to drag an innocent, unsuspecting woman into your life and pass yourself off as "available" simply because there's a void that needs to be filled. Yes, I get it. You're lonely. You want a companion. You desire sex. You need to replace your lost ticket into the world of couples. You don't know how to live life as a single man. You want to socialize with your married friends without feeling like the odd man out or a fifth wheel. You're humiliated by the pitying looks and feeble attempts of people to fix you up with every available woman they know.

These are all perfectly understandable reasons for wanting to be in a relationship, but you're giving little thought to the needs and feelings of the woman who unwittingly got sucked into all this baggage. It makes her feel like her main purpose is to fill an empty spot, to serve as a shock absorber for your grief, and to restore balance to your life. When she objects to your continued attachment to your late wife, she is often accused of being unreasonable and hard-hearted, or worse, jealous, insecure, and feeling threatened by a dead woman. In reality, her discontentment is an indication that she wants first place in your life and in your heart. If you continue hanging on to anything pertaining to your late wife, you're sending your current love interest the message that (a) she's not enough; (b) you liked your previous life better; and (c) she will never completely have all of your heart. That's a very harsh thing to do to a woman whose only crime is giving you another chance at love and happiness. There is no other situation in the world where a woman is subjected to intolerable conditions that would be considered deal breakers in other relationships.

You should NOT have your late wife's photo on your phone, the walls of your house, in your wallet, on Facebook, etc., no matter what the occasion or situation. This is tantamount to telling the next woman that your real true love is and always will be your late wife. It makes the woman in your life today feel like a placeholder or cheap filler. Look at it this way, how do you think your late wife would feel if SHE had to live in a house with another woman's photos and personal belongings in her face? I'd be willing to bet that you would have never considered keeping visible reminders of any of your ex-girlfriends around where your late wife had to see them all the time. You certainly would not expect her to be okay with it, either. Yet many girlfriends, fiancées, and wives of widowers not only have to live with photos of your late wife shoved down her throat, she may also be living with you in the house where you made a home with your late wife. This includes her décor, her personal belongings (clothing, shoes, accessories, cosmetics, toiletries, etc.). Yep, some widowers continue to hang on to everything that your late wives left behind and the woman who loves you and moves into this house feels like she is living in a shrine for the woman who came before her. If you are really ready to move forward and you truly love the woman in your life today, you would do whatever is necessary to make her feel happy, comfortable, and at home in your house.

Would YOU want to live with the woman you love in a house filled with tangible reminders of a guy she used to sleep with?

Another important situation that you need to act on is when your family or your late wife's relatives reject the woman in your life. She does not deserve to be treated like a piece of garbage. I understand that her presence is painful to those who loved your late wife, as well as a constant reminder that she's gone, but the woman you love today is not to blame for that. You need to get behind her and present a united front in order to put a lid on those "divide and conquer" tactics designed to put a wedge between the two of you. If you can't stand up to any opposition you receive from your kids or former in-laws, you're not ready for a relationship. It doesn't matter how "sensitive" or "emotional" they are about your being involved with another woman. They may never be ready to see you move on and you can't expect any self-respecting human being to take the brunt of somebody else's grief or hostility. You're either all in or you're not. Your late wife was never subjected to this type of abuse, and you wouldn't have tolerated anybody mistreating or subjecting her to these degrading indignities. The current woman in your life doesn't want any less than what her predecessor had, and rightfully so. So please, do yourself and your ladylove a favor and protect her from the stinging comments and actions coming from those who can't deal with the fact that you're moving on.

The new lady in your life should not be made to feel as if she's being selfish for wanting all of your heart that your late wife once had. There's nothing wrong with her walking away from you if you can't give her what she needs. She has the right to decide how she wants to fit into your life. If you want to wallow in your grief and stay in love with your late wife forever, have at it. Just don't expect any worthwhile woman to accept a relationship under these conditions. Your late wife's death was YOUR loss, not hers. She doesn't want to go along for the ride. Grieving is not a couple's activity. It's the same principle when people make excuses for being stuck or not getting ahead in life. They'll blame everything on a lousy childhood, dysfunctional family, or something else in their past. It happened. Everybody experiences pain and adversity. Either get over it and move on or get used to being by yourself. No self-respecting woman will settle for the leftover crumbs from your late wife's table.

Do yourself and your new woman another favor. Knock off the Facebook crap. News flash: Dead people don't read Facebook comments, so why in God's name would you ever post your late wife a "Happy Birthday, Valentine's Day, anniversary" message? She'll never see it, so who exactly would you be posting it for? What purpose does it serve? All it does is make you look like an attention whore and you're giving spiteful satisfaction to those who resent the new woman in your life. How can you possibly justify having an exclusive, intimate relationship with one woman while openly proclaiming your ongoing love for another woman who is no longer here? These publicly posted expressions of endearment directed at your late wife are like a stab in the heart to your current spouse or significant other, not to mention the anger and resentment it causes her. The woman in your life is giving you her love and a commitment while you're openly pining away for the woman who came before her. It's humiliating and categorically disrespectful. Just because your late wife is no longer here doesn't mean that her presence isn't felt, particularly when you're posting sentimental things on social media. Remove your widower label and you're still a man who needs to be loyal to the woman in your life.

If you are not ready to put that marriage behind you, the same as if you were divorced, then you are not ready for a relationship. The marriage vows are "til death do you part," and the next woman that you become seriously involved with deserves the right to be the ONLY woman in your heart. No woman should have to endure the pain of being in the shadow of anyone else, be it an ex-wife, former girlfriend, or even a late wife. The next woman does not need to see pictures, listen to stories, or be told that she needs to be put on a shelf for periods of time while you process unresolved grief. Worst of all, you're creating the impression that a woman's value increases after she dies.

If you cannot commit to your new woman entirely, by all means, be a man and let her know so she can choose to move on to somebody who can and will love her in the way she deserves. Don't lead her on, asking her to give you "more time to adjust." You should have straightened yourself out BEFORE you took it upon yourself to jump into another relationship. Don't use the next woman to ease the transition because you're unable to adapt to the single life. That's a very inconsiderate and self-centered act on your part. Yes, I know. Your late wife died and you miss her. I get that. But this is the hand that life dealt you. Either accept it and move on or stay in the past and resign yourself to being alone. I'm not suggesting that you shouldn't take all the time you need to recover from the loss of your late wife, but until you do, it's inconsiderate of you to get involved with the next woman just to get your needs met while keeping your heart on hold and being emotionally unavailable.

Are you hanging on to your late wife's ashes? What are you saving them for? The message you're sending to the woman who loves you is that you're keeping whatever physical remnants of your late wife that you can still have. Either spread them in a place your late wife liked to be or give them to your children or your former in-laws, but don't expect the woman you love to live among the dregs of your life from the past. Just get rid of the ashes and be done with it. Also, stay out of the cemetery. You may not think it takes anything away from the woman in your life by visiting your late wife's grave, but you're wrong. What your current woman feels when you go there is that your late wife is on your mind enough where you took the time to get into your car to make a trip to her gravesite. Nobody likes the feeling that the person they love is still dwelling on somebody else. How passionate do you think your woman feels when you keep wasting your time running back and forth to the cemetery to visit the final resting place of your late wife? Your current woman might just tell you to bring the ashes to bed with you or go to the cemetery to get your rocks off the next time you're feeling frisky. No decent, self-respecting woman will have any desire for you if she feels that you have an appetite for somebody else while coming to her for your meal. If you feel that your woman's desire for you is fading, you need to ask yourself why. It's not because she has no sex drive, or that she is not attracted to you, or no longer finds you appealing. It's because she can't love you with her body unless she feels like she's the only one on your mind and in your heart. Maybe sex is a physical thing for men, but for a woman, passion is emotional. A woman's desire for you begins from the neck up.

Just to be clear, the principles regarding ashes and cemetery visits do not apply to relatives or other loved ones who are no longer with us. So, don't try to level the playing field when the woman in your life hangs on to ashes or goes to the cemetery to visit deceased family members. Once a parent, grandparent, sibling, or (God forbid) a child, or other blood relative passes on, you will never be able to get another parent, child, sibling, to replace them. The same does not hold true for spouses and significant others. Nobody gets hurt by your attachment to dearly departed, blood related loved ones, but it's different when it comes to the late wife. The dynamics are not the same. You didn't sleep with Grandmom or Aunt Tillie. A romantic partner is a different kind of love that we can have more than once. This would be a very sad life, indeed, if we only got the chance to have one romantic partner in our lifetime. Fortunately, we do have the privilege of getting another opportunity to fall in love and be happy again. The human heart is resilient. Don't blow your chance with the next relationship by hanging on to a woman who is no longer here. There's just not enough room for the person you love today as well as the one you used to love. Three's a crowd and it's one heart too many.

Be careful not to use the word "we" when mentioning past memories. I realize that your late wife was probably a large part of your previous years, but it's not necessary to tell the woman in your life what "WE" did, meaning you and your late wife, when talking about something that happened before she came into the picture. Nothing wrong about sharing memories of past vacations, restaurants you went to, or whatever, but when doing so, you should speak in terms of "I" and "me" instead of "us" and "we." All this does is make the woman who loves you feel detached and segregated from the part of your life that didn't include her. It's not necessary to keep reminding the woman you love that you had a lot of history with someone who came before her. Trust me...she KNOWS.

The new woman in your life doesn't give a darn that "we" went to this restaurant; that "we" saw that movie; that "we" vacationed in Mexico; that "we" went on a cruise; if "we" loved that place. If you would just talk about YOUR experiences and interests and make it personal instead of about you and your late wife, it would be a lot easier for the next woman to listen to.

She also doesn't need to hear about how much your little Suzie looks exactly like her mother or that she takes after your late wife in certain ways. Stop bringing up the comparisons between your offspring and your late wife. The last thing she wants to see are living, breathing reminders of her everywhere she turns. We, too, as the new woman in a widower's life, have children who look or act like their fathers. We don't keep harping on the similarities between our own children and the man who came before you. We don't want to focus on visual manifestations of our former spouses and we certainly aren't interested in seeing anything reminiscent of the woman you once had an intimate relationship with. We have no desire to join you in your sentimental strolls down Memory Lane. Go there if you feel you must, but don't expect us to come along for the ride. We prefer to live in a state of reality, in the here and now. Stay in the present and let go of what no longer exists.

A woman has no interest in the part of your life spent with another woman. All this does is make the woman in your life wonder if you would choose to go back there with your late wife if you could and that you're only with her because you can't have your late wife. She doesn't need to know that you'd still be with her if she hadn't died; she needs to hear that given the choice, you'd stay right where you are even if you had the opportunity to have your late wife back again. She wants to feel that you are happy that she came into your life, regardless of how it happened.

Don't let your children take their pain out on the woman in your life. That means that you should never overcompensate for them. I cannot find words strong enough to describe how much heartache I have witnessed in women who are terribly mistreated by their widower's offspring. You're not doing your children any favors by going easy on them because their mother died. You're only training them to believe that the world is going to bend over backwards for them due to their grief, which encourages them to develop a warped sense of entitlement and a lifelong habit of bad manners. I realize that your relationship is a painful reminder that the mother they loved and lost is gone and that you're moving on with somebody else, but again, don't reward them when they play the grief or guilt card. It's a man's responsibility to stand up for and protect the woman he loves. Emotional and verbal abuse are just as stinging as a physical attack. Don't sit back and let your new woman be subjected to any kind of mistreatment that you would not expect your mother, sister, or daughter to tolerate from your children. Remember, the woman in your life is ALSO somebody's mother, sister, and daughter.

Whether your wife died expectedly after a lingering illness, a sudden accident, murder, suicide, or whatever, remember, it's not your fault. You did not cause her death, and you couldn't have prevented it. You're not powerful enough to manipulate Fate, so if you're feeling any sense of guilt or responsibility for her death, you need to shake it off and let it go. You have your own path to create and to follow. Your late wife's story is over. Her chapter in your life has ended and if the truth be told, it was really never your story to write — or to finish.

Lose the mood swings. Many widowers get into a funk when the late wife's date of death rolls around. The same often happens when it's her birthday, the day you met her, your wedding anniversary, and any other significant dates that are associated with your life with her. Your focus should be on your current woman's birthday, the day you met HER, and any other significant dates associated with the life you are living NOW. The significant dates from your life with your late wife should have no impact on you after you become involved with somebody else. If they still affect you, then you should resign yourself to being alone instead of dragging somebody else into your grief fest. Honestly, your new woman doesn't give a damn that you met Lucy on April 12 or if her birthday is December 6 or that you got married on June 20. Those dates are meaningless to her and the same should hold true for you. If you start moping around over a date associated with your late wife, it makes your new woman feel like you're longing for your late wife and that your new love isn't strong enough to offset what you once had. If you're going to get into a snit or become weepy and melancholy over these dates, just remember that these memories aren't going to provide you with companionship or keep you warm at night if the woman who loves you gets so fed up with this nonsense that she decides to unload you. If you keep this crap up, you'll end up flying solo again, and this time, it will be your own doing. Appreciate what you have instead of wasting your time dwelling on what you lost. Are you so self-centered that you believe that your pain and loss is any worse than what your current woman feels over her own dearly departed loved ones? She, too, has experienced sorrow and the death of loved ones in the course of her own life. She doesn't need to get sucked into yours, ESPECIALLY over another woman.

Maybe you have guilt that stems from the fact that you mistreated your late wife in some way, cheated on her, or whatever. People make mistakes. You are human. You have to give up hope for a better past. No matter how much you beat yourself up, you cannot go back and rewrite your history. You can make your best amends to your late wife by learning from your mistakes and becoming a better man for the next woman. There is absolutely no purpose to be served by punishing yourself for the rest of your life.

Put the current woman in your life FIRST. She is your partner now and should come before everybody, especially and including your former in-laws. I realize that it could be hurtful to them to see another woman with a place in your life that used to belong to their dearly departed loved one, but they need to accept that you're with somebody else now. It is very important to the woman you're with to feel that building a life with her is far more important to you than your connections to the past.

Don't compartmentalize and segregate. This is important when your friends, children, and others in your life do not accept your current spouse or partner. If you receive an invitation that does not include her...don't go. I am not referring to a guys' day or night out when you go to a ballgame with your buddies or something of that nature. I'm talking about wedding invitations, holiday celebrations, birthday parties, and other events where people always attend with their spouses or significant others. If you accept an invitation that was not extended to her, you're encouraging others to exclude her and letting them know that you will tolerate it. Also, if you and your significant other send cards and gifts in both your names and then you receive a "thank you" note addressed only to you, don't give another gift or card to anybody who doesn't acknowledge and include your partner in their "thank you" note. This is ill-mannered and blatantly disrespectful to her. The two of you need to present a united front — always. Others must understand that if they don't include your spouse or significant other, then you won't bother with them. They need to see your respect for her and your commitment to the relationship. If they want to be a part of your life, they must include her and treat her kindly and not with forced, tolerated civility.

Let go of any guilt you may be feeling about being happy. You may be asking yourself why you get to live and have another chance to fall in love and enjoy life again when your late wife can't. We are not meant to know how and why everything happens in this life. For whatever the reason, she's gone and you're still here. Become the best man you can be, and going forward, leave a positive impact on those who cross your path. Make it count.

Finally, open your heart freely and fully to love and happiness again. Embrace life completely with everything you have and take a leap of faith into a better future. Don't be afraid to jump in. The water is fine!

Printed in Great Britain
by Amazon

66619395R00095